SpringerBriefs in Computer Science

More information about this series at http://www.springer.com/series/10028

Kim J.L. Nevelsteen

A Survey of Characteristic Engine Features for Technology-Sustained Pervasive Games

Kim J.L. Nevelsteen
Deparment of Computer and Systems Sciences
Stockholm University
Stockholm, Sweden

ISSN 2191-5768   ISSN 2191-5776   (electronic)
SpringerBriefs in Computer Science
ISBN 978-3-319-17631-4   ISBN 978-3-319-17632-1   (eBook)
DOI 10.1007/978-3-319-17632-1

Library of Congress Control Number: 2015938304

Springer Cham Heidelberg New York Dordrecht London

Printed on acid-free paper

Springer International Publishing AG Switzerland is part of Springer Science+Business Media (www.
springer.com)

To Charlie Brown,
my high school English teacher,
who carried a long stick,
had a daughter, and lots of leg hair.

Acknowledgments

Sincerest gratitude to Theo Kanter, Rahim Rahmani, and Annika Waern for their guidance; Jakob Axelsson, Leif Oppermann, Jim Wilenius, and Newton Lee for their critical reviews; Karl-Petter Åkesson for providing details on IPerG in his spare time; Todd Sundsted for offering his intricate knowledge about LambdaMOO; and, not least, Mama for her endless support.

Research was made possible by a grant from the Swedish Governmental Agency for Innovation Systems to the Mobile Life Vinn Excellence Center.

Contents

Acronyms

ARG   Alternate Reality Game, a subgenre of pervasive game (see Sect. 1.5)

AR   Augmented Reality, a technique for overlaying the physical world with virtual content

CYSMN   Can You See Me Now?, a surveyed pervasive game from the Equator collaboration (see Sect. 2.2.1.1)

CN:H   Codename: Heroes, pervasive game created in the case study of Chap. 3 (see Sect. 3.2)

DEVAL   Device Abstraction Layer, abstraction layer to handle the heterogeneity of devices (see Sect. 2.2.2.2)

ECT   EQUIP Component Toolkit, component extending EQUIP, designed to deal with the heterogeneity of devices (see Sect. 2.2.1.1)

EQUIP   Equator 'Universal Platform', an extensible middleware platform for both CYSMN and URAY (see Sect. 2.2.1.1)

FinN   Fun in Numbers, a platform which was surveyed (see Sect. 2.2.7)

GIS   Geographic Information System, a system designed to handle all types of spatial or geographical data

GM   Game Master, person(s) responsible of adjusting the game during its staging (see Sect. 1.6)

GPS   Global Positioning System, a space-based satellite positioning system

IPerG   Integrated Project on Pervasive Gaming, one of the large collaborations of the survey (see Sect. 2.2.2)

LARP   Live Action Role Play, when technology-supported, a subgenre of pervasive games (see Sect. 1.5)

LPMUD   Lars Pensjö MUD, a type of MUD game engine in the MU*/MOO family of architectures used in Ambient Wood (see Sect. 2.2.1.2)

MEAP   MUD-Elvin Application Proxy, message relaying component used in Ambient Wood (see Sect. 2.2.1.2)

MCP   MUD Client Protocol, network communication protocol used in CN:H (see Sect. 3.4.3)

MUD   Multi-User Dungeon, virtual world engine first implemented in 1978, referred to as MUD1 (see Sect. 3.3)

MOO   LambdaMOO, virtual world engine in the MU*/MOO family of architectures used in CN:H (see Sect. 3.3)

MUPE   Multi-User Publishing Environment, a client/server component used in
Mythical Mobile (see Sect. 2.2.2.1)

NPC   Non-Player Character, characters in a game not directly controlled by a
player, see Index

PART   Pervasive Applications RunTime, a light-weight middleware used in
Interference (see Sect. 2.2.2.2)

PIMP   Pervasive Interactive Mobile Platform, a component supporting heterogeneous devices used in Interference (see Sect. 2.2.2.2)

STARS   not an acronym, a platform from the survey (see Sect. 2.2.6)

URAY   Uncle Roy All Around You, a surveyed pervasive game from the
Equator collaboration (see Sect. 2.2.1.1)

WAF   Web Application Framework, component used in Mythical Mobile (see
Sect. 2.2.2.1)

WOz   'Wizard of Oz' technique for testing an architecture (see Sect. 2.3.8)

WLAN   Wireless Local Area Network, networking often based on the IEEE
802.11 standards, sometimes referred to as Wi-Fi

Chapter 1
Pervasive Games with Persistent Worlds

1.1 Introduction

According to Benford, Magerkurth, and Ljungstrand (2005), if traditional games have game elements in the physical world and computer games have game elements in the virtual, then "pervasive games extend the gaming experience out into the real [physical] world", with a representation of game elements in the physical, the virtual or a blend of both. Because the domain of pervasive games is broad and imprecise (Nieuwdorp, 2007), the focus of this book will be on pervasive games that satisfy the sub-domain criteria: pervasive games that *make use of virtual game elements*. In her definitive work, Nieuwdorp (2007, original italics) derives that pervasive games can be discussed from two perspectives, a technological one, "that focuses on computing technology *as a tool to enable the game to come into being*" or a cultural one, "that focuses on *the game itself*". This book is requirements and development-focused Design Science research (Johannesson & Perjons, 2014) examining pervasive games from a technological perspective, under the assumption that the technology utilized determines a set of pervasive games that can be supported from a cultural perspective e.g., position localization technologies enable location-based games.

According to Broll, Ohlenburg, Lindt, Herbst, and Braun (2006), game engines for pervasive games do not differ entirely from computer games engines, because "while the overall game is a mixed reality application combining the real [physical] and the virtual, the game engine actually does not need to be aware of this fact". Paelke, Oppermann, and Reimann (2008) suggest a web server to stand as pervasive game engine. In the computer game industry, the use of a game engine to build games is common; the major incentive for employing a reusable game engine being reduced development time and cost (Lewis & Jacobson, 2002; Bass, Clements, & Kazman, 2013). If pervasive games are to reap the same benefits, then engines for pervasive games must be available (Paelke et al., 2008). But, current computer game

© The Author(s) 2015
K.J.L. Nevelsteen, *A Survey of Characteristic Engine Features for Technology-Sustained Pervasive Games*, SpringerBriefs in Computer Science, DOI 10.1007/978-3-319-17632-1_1

engines do not support pervasive games that move the game beyond the computer screen, out into the physical world, unbound by scheduled play times and possibly involving unknowing bystanders i.e., games that are expanded spatially, temporally and/or socially. Since the computer game industry is already rich with engines and game engines can be repurposed beyond their intended use (Lewis & Jacobson, 2002) (e.g., the use of the Quake (id Software, 1996) engine in the augmented reality game, called ARQuake (Oppermann, 2009)), this book investigates: (i) if a game engine can be repurposed to stage pervasive games; (ii) if features describing a would-be pervasive game engine can be identified; (iii) using those features, if an architecture be found in the same 'product line' (Bass et al., 2013) as an existing engine and if that architecture can be extended to stage pervasive games (iv) and, finally, if there any challenges and open issues that remain.

The approach to answering these questions is two fold: First, a survey of pervasive games is conducted, gathering technical details and features of various games, projects and technologies (see Chap. 2). Approaches, technologies and overall goals of each of the surveyed projects could differ greatly, including their aim to create either game-specific engines or more universal solutions. To stay within scope of the book, only those projects supporting the sub-domain criteria were considered. The gathered features are distilled into a component feature set that enables pervasive games and verified e.g., against the definitions of pervasive games and in comparison to related work. Second, a type of game engine is chosen (supporting as much of the feature set as possible) as candidate in the same product line as a would-be pervasive game engine. The architecture is extended to support the entire feature set and used to stage a pervasive game called Codename: Heroes (CN:H) as proof-of-concept (see Chap. 3). From the outset CN:H had the requirement of being a 'long term pervasive game', emphasizing 'stability' and 'scalability' by using a 'mature' (ISO, 2011) engine. Limited resources called for rapid development and using a game engine would allow designers to immediately implement the game play instead of implementation mechanics (Branton, Carver, & Ullmer, 2011; Suomela, Räsänen, Koivisto, & Mattila, 2004). Implementing CN:H serves to validate the architecture and give needed first-hand experience with the resulting architecture. Whereas features from the survey informed the architecture, the implementation of CN:H served to highlight those features of particular importance and identify any open issues.

Before presenting the survey in Chap. 2 and the case study in Chap. 3, the following sections contain: what a game engine is and its purpose; how game, physical and virtual worlds relate; a clarification pertaining to the ambiguities of persistence, in relation to the worlds and the game engine; a definition of pervasive games; and, an explanation of the three different temporal phases of staging a pervasive game.

1.2 Game Engine

When referring to a game's *architecture*, this can refer to both the software and hardware supporting the game. In order to divide-and-conquer complexity and promote reuse, software can be divided into components ('modules' (Bass et al., 2013)) that enable common features. A collection of components can be organized into a software architecture, which can be used as a game engine. Core functionality is often compiled into the game engine for performance reasons (Gregory, 2009). An engine can be data-driven,[1] with functionality (including the engine configuration) controlled through a scripting language (Gregory, 2009; Branton et al., 2011), alleviating the need for core engine programmers (Gregory, 2009; Greenhalgh, Izadi, Mathrick, Humble, & Taylor, 2004). The term *game engine* is sometimes used interchangeably with more specialized engines, such as a graphics engine, physics engine, virtual world engine, augmented reality[2] engine or middleware (Gregory, 2009). Gregory (2009) states the definition of a game engine to be "software that is extensible and can be used as the foundation for many different games without major modification". The more 'universal' (Gregory, 2009) an engine is, the more games can be supported (Hall & Novak, 2008; Lewis & Jacobson, 2002).

The benefits of using a game engine are reduced development time and cost. One way to reduce development cost, is to reduce the amount of code written, by reusing code e.g., if the cost of acquiring the engine far outweighs the development cost to implement the same feature set (Hall & Novak, 2008). Reduced development time is made possible by the engine, because designers are able to immediately start work on the actual game, while other components are still under development (Gregory, 2009; Lewis & Jacobson, 2002; Greenhalgh et al., 2004; Hall & Novak, 2008), satisfying both designers and technology experts (Paelke et al., 2008). If pervasive games are to reap the benefits of reduced development time and cost, then engines for pervasive games must be available.

1.3 Worlds

Various types of *worlds* are discussed in this book, qualified by the descriptors: game, physical or virtual. The abstract notion of a *game world*, according to Adams and Rollings (2006), is a reality created by pretending: "when the player enters the

---

[1]"The behavior of a game can be controlled, in whole or in part, by *data* provided by artists and designers rather than exclusively by *software* produced by programmers" (Gregory, 2009, original italics).

[2]A system combining the virtual and the physical enabling a real-time interactive three dimensional environment (Oppermann, 2009).

magic circle [the contractual magic circle of play, according to Montola, Stenros, and Waern (2009)] and pretends to be somewhere else, the game world is the place she pretends to be". The term *physical world* shall be used throughout the book, rather than 'real world' or 'reality', to avoid the discussion on what is real or not.[3] And lastly, to avoid entering the discourse on what a *virtual world* is (M. W. Bell, 2008), it is to be understood here as: minimally, a spatiotemporal instance with interacting virtual elements[4] in the instance, where one or more of the elements could be a representation of a player. Temporality in the instance allows for change.

If the game world the player pretends to be in, overlaps with the virtual or the physical, then at least some of the game elements must be present in the virtual or physical, respectively. A mixed representation is possible, but to exactly what extent the physical and virtual can overlap is beyond the scope of this book. If a game element exists in the physical, it may or may not have a virtual counterpart, and vice versa. If the game world overlaps with the physical, the gaming experience is extended out in the physical world, with the game world being part of a pervasive game.

1.4 Persistence

The term *persistence* is often used in conjunction with a virtual world (James et al., 2004), but is ambiguous. To resolve the ambiguity here, persistence is divided into three components: world, data and network. It is also possible to speak of a persistent game world, but aside from the three components, persisting a game world is from a done from a cultural perspective.

For a virtual world, *world persistence* refers to an environment that "continues to exist and develop internally even when there are no people interacting with it" (Bartle, 2003). The physical world is persistent and since pervasive games can blend with the physical, pervasive games are persistent worlds, sharing the trait of a persistence with virtual worlds (de Souza e Silva & Sutko, 2009a). In pervasive games, exact times of play (when the player is in the game world) can be expanded temporally, making times "remain uncertain, ambiguous, and hard to define" (Montola et al., 2009). A solution is to make the game world available at all times, as suggested by one of the definitions of pervasive games, "a game with a persistent presence in the real [physical] world, and thus available to the players at all times" (Nieuwdorp, 2007). Another solution is to simulate world persistence, by either scheduling play times around when the world is unavailable or by making relevant player/world data available at least when those player(s) reconnect to the game (Söderlund, 2009). To simulate a world developing internally, change can be generated relative to how much time has elapsed since the players connected.

---

[3]"Reality is that which, when you stop believing in it, doesn't go away" (Dick, 1978).

[4]Virtual elements are elements simulated by computers (Bartle, 2003; M. W. Bell, 2008).

If the game state (including player records, game objects,[5] or other data) maintained by the game engine, is said to be contained in its *data space* (Greenhalgh, Izadi, Rodden, & Benford, 2001), *data persistence* aims to ensure the preservation of the data space in the event of a shutdown or system failure i.e., ensuring 'fault tolerance' and 'recoverability' (ISO, 2011). The persistence requirement by James et al. (2004), stating that the world "retains records of player data indefinitely", corresponds to data persistence. If the data space is partially or entirely held in computer memory, data persistence can be achieved by writing out the data space to non-volatile storage e.g., in the form of a flat file or to a database. Contrary to persistence, when the state of the world is not critical, the game state can be left in volatile memory, providing neither fault tolerance or recoverability; the engine is restarted in the event of failure.

The last form persistence discussed is that of persistent connectivity or *network persistence* (Ståhl, Drozd, Greenhalgh, & Koivisto, 2006). But, considering pervasive games must contend with lots of uncertainty in connectivity (Oppermann, 2009) (see Sect. 2.3.4), network persistence is often not possible and something that is strived towards. In an attempt to take advantage of uncertainty, in the game called Treasure (M. Bell, 2007), the disconnected state was used as a game mechanic.

1.5   Pervasive Games

Although the origins of ubiquitous computing and pervasive computing differ (Nieuwdorp, 2007), they are often used interchangeably (Nieuwdorp, 2007; Montola, 2012) and are both the basis for pervasive gaming (Nieuwdorp, 2007). According to Montola (2012), "a pervasive game is a game that has one or more salient features that expand the contractual magic circle of play spatially, temporally or socially". Montola (2012) goes on to recognize the definitive work by Nieuwdorp (2007), wherein the various meanings of pervasive games are summarized e.g., games that: depend on non-standard input devices,[6] are augmented by computers, blend the physical and virtual, or have a persistent presence in the physical world. It is precisely the definitions by Nieuwdorp (2007), that the feature set will be verified against in Sect. 2.5.

The term *pervasive game* has been associated with a number of subgenres: ubiquitous games, augmented/mixed reality games, alternate reality games, (enhanced) live action role play (E/LARP), virtual reality games, location-based games and

---

[5]"The collection of object types that make up a game is called the *game object model*. The game object model provides a real-time simulation of a heterogeneous collection of objects in the virtual game world" (Gregory, 2009, original italics).

[6]"A device is a combination of a hardware component and a software component, sending or receiving data. The software component may contain a driver, a library, or a software development kit" (Appelt, Ohlenburg, Greenhalgh, Oppermann, & Åkesson, 2008).

more (Nieuwdorp, 2007). Instead of focusing on a particular subgenre, the focus of this book is on the sub-domain of pervasive games, that satisfy the sub-domain criteria of: pervasive games that make use of virtual game elements. Such a minimal criteria means, games satisfying the sub-domain criteria might exist in several of the subgenres. The sub-domain was chosen as a minimum, to specify that computer simulation is used to support the game world of the pervasive game. The sub-domain is important to limit the scope of the survey in Chap. 2. Examples of games that fail to satisfy the sub-domain criteria are some ARGs or LARPs, which are perhaps technology-supported, but are not technology-sustained (Montola et al., 2009) i.e., have no need for a game engine.

1.6   Staging a Pervasive Game

Ståhl, Ohlenburg, Greenhalgh, and Nenonen (2007) have identified three temporal phases in staging a pervasive game: 'pre-production', 'run-time' and 'post-production'. Because these phases concern games, these phases have also been referred to as 'pre-game', 'in-game', and 'post-game' (Jonsson, Waern, Montola, & Stenros, 2007; Broll et al., 2006). The latter convention is used throughout this book, reserving *run-time* to refer to when a game architecture is running and *in-game* to refer to when the game is running. In the *pre-game* phase, although resource demanding (M. Bell, 2007), a game can potentially be adapted to each new staging (e.g., adapting to a new staging location (Oppermann, 2009) i.e., supporting *location adaptability*). Adapting the game is done through reconfiguring the architecture and authoring content specific to each staging. Reconfiguration and authoring can continue into the in-game phase, provided it is supported by the architecture. In the *post-game* phase, an analysis of historic event data can be performed, players debriefed and informed to the actual flow events (Stenros, Montola, Waern, & Jonsson, 2007b). The results of a post-game analysis can inform further game design or stagings.

One of the driving factors why current game engines are ill suited for pervasive games is game mastering. Contrary to many video games, pervasive games do not necessarily run fully automatic. One or more persons, often referred to as *game master(s)* (GMs), can be assigned the responsibility of adjusting the game during its staging; an act which is referred to as *game mastering* (Jonsson & Waern, 2008; Oppermann, 2009; Montola et al., 2009) or *orchestration* (Thompson, Weal, Michaelides, Cruickshank, & Roure, 2003; Flintham, Anastasi, et al., 2003; Broll et al., 2006). A well known role for a game master is that of a 'puppet master'; in charge and 'pulling strings', all the while staying hidden behind the scenes (Jonsson & Waern, 2008). Jonsson and Waern (2008) have argued that pervasive games benefit from being game-mastered e.g., allowing for: content to be actively authored to "fit the activities of the participants"; the altering of game events, adjusting of difficulty, providing dynamic gameplay or the reincorporating of user response back into the game (Jonsson et al., 2007). Because pervasive games take place in the physical world, another responsibility of the game master is to keep players safe in the highly variable, possibly dangerous conditions of the physical world (Flintham, Anastasi, et al., 2003; Broll et al., 2006). A drawback of game mastering being that it can require a significant amount of human resources (Thompson et al., 2003; Flintham, Benford, et al., 2003). Jonsson and Waern (2008) have identified three needed functions, in order to successfully game master: (1) to be able to monitor the game, (2) make decisions about how the game should progress, and (3) have the ability to influence the game state.

1.6.1   Monitoring the Game

Players of pervasive games are mobile and out in the physical world. Two ways to monitor a player are: stationary hardware placed in the physical world (Stenros, Montola, Waern, & Jonsson, 2007a; Jonsson & Waern, 2008) or by giving players mobile devices to carry, interact and communicate with (Jonsson & Waern, 2008; Montola et al., 2009). The physical world affords seemingly infinite possibilities, meaning players are always able to produce 'soft' events, outside the awareness of the game architecture, but still in relation to the game (Jonsson & Waern, 2008). To capture some of these soft events, players can be monitored through direct surveillance and accounts thereof registered in game architecture (Crabtree et al., 2004; Montola et al., 2009). To assist in picking up on soft events, players can also be tasked with self-reporting, in the form of diaries (Montola et al., 2009; Jonsson et al., 2007).

Perhaps not part of the game state, per say, but important in monitoring a game mastered game, is any meta-level information e.g., game master notes instructing other game masters on the state of the game (Montola et al., 2009).

1.6.2   Support Decision Making

To support game master decision making in-game, the potentially massive amounts of event information during monitoring must be dealt with. Additional information to aid decision making includes semi-static information, such as player information (e.g., photo, contact details, emergency information, game relevant skills) or documented help on how to stage a specific event (Jonsson et al., 2007). Automation aids game masters in decision making (Bartle, 2003), but obviously reduces game mastering, leading increasingly to a fully automated experience. One option to reduce game master load, without increasing automation, is to provide support tools e.g., in the form of specialized GM interfaces or log analysis tools (Montola et al., 2009; Broll et al., 2006; Dow et al., 2005). Support tools convert or condense event information into a human consumable format. Another option is to cast non-player characters (NPCs) (de Souza e Silva & Sutko, 2009b) in, to offload game master responsibilities (Jonsson & Waern, 2008) achieving a more decentralized orchestration (Crabtree et al., 2004). Once game masters have made decisions, each decision must be actuated into the game.

1.6.3   Influencing the Game State

A common way to actuate change in a system, in run-time, is to directly alter the internal state of the game engine i.e., alter variables in the game's data space (provided it is possible to access it) (Jonsson et al., 2007; Jonsson & Waern, 2008; Hansson, Åkesson, & Wallberg, 2007; Broll et al., 2006). Depending on the architecture, not all modifications are possible in run-time and in such a situation, the system must be brought offline to make necessary modifications (Hansson et al., 2007). Manually manipulating variables in the data space can be cumbersome when authoring lots of content. Developers of a game can attempt to anticipate what part of the data space game masters need access to and build an appropriate GM interface to it.

Although important for relaying observed events in monitoring a game, communication also plays an important role in influencing the game state e.g., by pushing information directly to the players (Jonsson & Waern, 2008). Communication can be either *diegetic*[7] or non-diegetic (Bergström, 2011), with the non-diegetic channel being particularly important to communicate out of the context of the game, in case of emergencies (Jonsson & Waern, 2008). Communication channels can be uni- or bi-directional.

References

Adams, E., & Rollings, A. (2006). *Fundamentals of game design (game design and development series)*. Upper Saddle River, NJ, USA: Prentice-Hall, Inc.
Appelt, W., Ohlenburg, J., Greenhalgh, C., Oppermann, L., & Åkesson, K.-P. (2008, April). *Deliverable D7.7: final software delivery of WP 7*.
Bartle, R. (2003). *Designing virtual worlds*. Indianapolis, Indiana, USA: New Riders Publishing.
Bass, L., Clements, P., & Kazman, R. (2013). *Software architecture in practice* (3rd). Addison-Wesley Professional.
Bell, M. (2007). *Guidelines and infrastructure for the design and implementation of highly adaptive, context-aware, mobile, peer-to-peer systems*. (Doctoral dissertation, University of Glasgow, Faculty of Information and Mathematical Sciences, Department of Computing Science).
Bell, M. W. (2008, July). Toward a definition of "virtual worlds". *Journal of Virtual Worlds Research, 1* (1).

---

[7]"The 'diegesis' of a story consists of whatever is true *in that story*. Diegetic elements are 'in the story'; non-diegetic elements are not." (Bergström, 2011, original italics)

Benford, S., Magerkurth, C., & Ljungstrand, P. (2005). Bridging the physical and digital in pervasive gaming. *Communications of the ACM, 48* (3), 54–57.

Bergström, K. (2011). Framing storytelling with games. In *Interactive storytelling* (pp. 170–181). Lecture Notes in Computer Science. Vancouver, Canada: Springer Berlin Heidelberg.

Branton, C., Carver, D., & Ullmer, B. (2011). Interoperability standards for pervasive games. In *Proceedings of the 1st international workshop on games and software engineering* (pp. 40–43). New York, NY, USA: ACM.

Broll, W., Ohlenburg, J., Lindt, I., Herbst, I., & Braun, A.-K. (2006, October). Meeting technology challenges of pervasive augmented reality games. In *Proceedings of 5th ACM SIGCOMM workshop on network and system support for games* (p. 28). Singapore: ACM.

Crabtree, A., Benford, S., Rodden, T., Greenhalgh, C., Flintham, M., Anastasi, R., . . . Steed, A. (2004). Orchestrating a mixed reality game 'on the ground'. In *Proceedings of the SIGCHI conference on human factors in computing systems* (pp. 391–398). CHI '04. Vienna, Austria: ACM.

de Souza e Silva, A., & Sutko, D. M. (2009a). Digital cityscapes. (Chap. Merging Digital and Urban Playspaces: An introduction to the Field, pp. 1–20). USA: Peter Lang.

de Souza e Silva, A., & Sutko, D. M. (Eds.). (2009b). *Digital cityscapes.* USA: Peter Lang.

Dick, P. K. (1978). *How to build a universe that doesn't fall apart two days later.* Retrieved from http://deoxy.org/pkd_how2build.htm

Dow, S., Lee, J., Oezbek, C., MacIntyre, B., Bolter, J. D., & Gandy, M. (2005). Wizard of oz interfaces for mixed reality applications. In *CHI '05 extended abstracts on human factors in computing systems* (pp. 1339–1342). New York, NY, USA: ACM.

Flintham, M., Anastasi, R., Benford, S., Drozd, A., Mathrick, J., Rowland, D., . . . Sutton, J. (2003, November). Uncle roy all around you: mixing games and theatre on the city streets. In *Level up conference proceedings.* University of Utrecht: DiGRA.

Flintham, M., Benford, S., Anastasi, R., Hemmings, T., Crabtree, A., Greenhalgh, C., . . . Row-Farr, J. (2003, April). Where on-line meets on the streets: experiences with mobile mixed reality games. In *Proceedings of the SIGCHI conference on human factors in computing systems* (pp. 569–576). CHI '03. New York, NY, USA: ACM.

Greenhalgh, C., Izadi, S., Mathrick, J., Humble, J., & Taylor, I. (2004, September). ECT: a toolkit to support rapid construction of ubicomp environments. In *Proceedings of workshop on system support for ubiquitous computing.* UbiSys. Nottingham, UK: Springer Verlag.

Greenhalgh, C., Izadi, S., Rodden, T., & Benford, S. (2001). *The EQUIP platform: bringing together physical and virtual worlds.*

Gregory, J. (2009, July). *Game engine architecture* (J. Lander & M. Whiting, Eds.). Wellesley, Massachusetts: A K Peters.

Hall, R., & Novak, J. (2008, April). *Game development essentials: online game development.* Clifton Park, NY, USA: Delmar Cengage Learning.

Hansson, P., Åkesson, K.-P., & Wallberg, A. (2007, February). *Deliverable D11.9: second generation core platform.*

id Software. (1996). Quake.

ISO. (2011). *ISO/IEC 25010:2011 systems and software engineering – systems and software quality requirements and evaluation (SQuaRE) – system and software quality models.*

James, D., Walton, G., Mills, G., Welch, J., Valadares, J., Estanislao, J., & DeBenedictis, S. (2004). *2004 persistent worlds whitepaper.*

Johannesson, P., & Perjons, E. (2014). *An introduction to design science.* Springer International Publishing Switzerland.

Jonsson, S., & Waern, A. (2008). Art of game-mastering pervasive games, the. In *Proceedings of the 2008 international conference on advances in computer entertainment technology* (pp. 224–231). ACE '08. New York, NY, USA: ACM.

Jonsson, S., Waern, A., Montola, M., & Stenros, J. (2007, June). Game mastering a pervasive larp. experiences from Momentum. In *Proceedings of the 4th international symposium on pervasive gaming applications* (pp. 31–39). Salzburg, Austria: PerGames.

Lewis, M., & Jacobson, J. (2002, January). Game engines in scientific research. *Communications of the ACM, 45* (1), 27–31.

Montola, M. (2012, September). *On the edge of the magic circle: understanding pervasive games and role-playing.* (Doctoral dissertation, School of Information Sciences).

Montola, M., Stenros, J., & Waern, A. (2009). *Pervasive games. theory and design. experiences on the boundary between life and play.* Burlington, MA, USA: Morgan Kaufmann Publishers.

Nieuwdorp, E. (2007, April). The pervasive discourse: an analysis. *Computers in Entertainment (CIE), 5.*

Oppermann, L. (2009, April). *Facilitating the development of location-based experiences.* (Doctoral dissertation, The University of Nottingham).

Paelke, V., Oppermann, L., & Reimann, C. (2008). Mobile location-based gaming. In *Map-based mobile services- design, interaction and usability* (Chap. 15, pp. 310–334). Springer Berlin Heidelberg.

Söderlund, T. (2009). Digital cityscapes. (Chap. Proximity Gaming: New Forms of Wireless Networking Gaming, pp. 217–250). USA: Peter Lang.

Ståhl, O., Drozd, A., Greenhalgh, C., & Koivisto, A. (2006, August). *Deliverable D6.7: second phase release of the IPerG platforms.*

Ståhl, O., Ohlenburg, J., Greenhalgh, C., & Nenonen, V. (2007, August). *Deliverable D6.8: final release of the IPerG platforms.*

Stenros, J., Montola, M., Waern, A., & Jonsson, S. (2007a, May). *Deliverable D11.8 appendix c: momentum evaluation report.*

Stenros, J., Montola, M., Waern, A., & Jonsson, S. (2007b). Play it for real: sustained seamless life/game merger in momentum. In *Situated play* (pp. 121–129). Tokyo, Japan: DiGRA.

Suomela, R., Räsänen, E., Koivisto, A., & Mattila, J. (2004). Open-source game development with the multi-user publishing environment (MUPE) application platform. In *Entertainment computing – ICEC 2004* (pp. 308–320). Eindhoven, The Netherlands: Springer Berlin Heidelberg.

Thompson, M. K., Weal, M. J., Michaelides, D. T., Cruickshank, D. G., & Roure, D. C. D. (2003). *MUD slinging: virtual orchestration of physical interactions.* ECSTRIAM03-007.

Chapter 2
Survey of Pervasive Games and Technologies

2.1 A Systematic Review

The survey aims to be a systematic review (Ampatzoglou & Stamelos, 2010) of existing pervasive games and their technologies, using purposive combined with snowball sampling (Johannesson & Perjons, 2014) and an inclusion/exclusion criteria equal to the sub-domain criteria.

The survey spans:
two large collaborations that together span 10 years:

- Equator, which brought together eight different institutions to research "inter-relationships between the physical and the digital" (EQUATOR, 2010), and
- IPerG, a collaboration of industry and academic partners (Steve Benford, Magerkurth, & Ljungstrand, 2005) to research a "new game form that extends gaming experiences out into the physical world" (IPerG, 2008);

two books pertaining to pervasive games:

- *Digital Cityscapes, merging digital and urban playspaces* (de Souza e Silva & Sutko, 2009a), and
- *Pervasive Games, Theory and Design, Experiences on the Boundary Between Life and Play* (Montola, Stenros, & Waern, 2009);

and, top ranking (first 100+) keyword search results, on Google Scholar, after the year 2009, for pervasive game: 'technology', 'architecture' or 'engine'. Complementary searches were performed to find references, citing previously found references, that were considered key to the study (e.g., Montola et al., 2009; de Souza e Silva & Sutko, 2009a; Nieuwdorp, 2007; Branton, Carver, & Ullmer, 2011; Broll, Ohlenburg, Lindt, Herbst, & Braun, 2006; Greenhalgh, Izadi, Mathrick, Humble, & Taylor, 2001, 2004) or referenced by Nieuwdorp (2007), relevant to the definition of pervasive games. Although there are plenty of publications on

© The Author(s) 2015   11
K.J.L. Nevelsteen, *A Survey of Characteristic Engine Features for Technology-Sustained Pervasive Games*, SpringerBriefs in Computer Science, DOI 10.1007/978-3-319-17632-1_2

pervasive games, it seems the majority are from a cultural perspective, with literature from a technological perspective being scarce or brief i.e., clarifying the need to reference tech reports rather than publications e.g., Appelt, Ohlenburg, Greenhalgh, Oppermann, and Åkesson (2008), Becam, Milding, Nenonen, Nummenmaa, and Kuittinen (2008), Holopainen (2008a, 2008b), Ståhl, Ohlenburg, Greenhalgh, and Nenonen (2007), Greenhalgh et al. (2001), Hansson, Åkesson, and Wallberg (2007), Stenros, Montola, Waern, and Jonsson (2007), Waern, Bichard, Boss, and Åkesson (2008), Waern, Lindt, Wetzel, and Åkesson (2008), Thompson, Weal, Michaelides, Cruickshank, and Roure (2003), Larsson (2006), and Freeman (2004).

A total of 59 pervasive games/projects and 27 technologies were surveyed (see Appendix A), simultaneously uncovering related work (discussed in Sect. 2.4). Games were excluded if a game engine was irrelevant e.g., although an engine could automate features, Killer (Montola et al., 2009) can be played without the need of a game engine, and games such as The Beast, Shelby Logan's Run and Vem Gråter (Montola et al., 2009) can be game mastered by placing puzzles on different media such as: TV, Internet, radio, etc. Also, games without sufficient documentation could not be included e.g., Ingress.[1]

2.2 Pervasive Games/Projects and Technologies

For brevity, rather than report on all games surveyed with many overlapping features, games reported in this section form a minimal set of games exhibiting all features of the resulting set. For each reported game, there is a section introducing, the game from a cultural perspective and any technologies that were used. As a conclusion, a component features set, considered central to supporting pervasive games is distilled and the games are discussed again, but from a technological perspective, in relation to different component features (in Sect. 2.3).

2.2.1 Equator IRC

The Equator Interdisciplinary Research Collaboration was a 6 year endeavor, started on October 2000. Equator projects were divided into a number of 'experiences'. Most of the projects in Equator do not satisfy the inclusion/exclusion criteria, but the 'Citywide Performance', 'Playing and Learning' and 'Seamful Games' experiences contribute heavily due to their use of heterogeneous devices. From the 'Citywide Performance' experience (Izadi et al., 2002), Can You See Me Now?

---

[1]At the time of this writing, John Hanke, leader of Niantic Labs, has posted an Internet article clarifying that Ingress architecture is client/server, including some design aspects from a cultural perspective (Hanke & Geiger, 2015).

(CYSMN) (Crabtree et al., 2004; Steve Benford et al., 2005; Flintham et al., 2003; Montola et al., 2009; Oppermann, 2009) and Uncle Roy All Around You (URAY) (Flintham, Anastasi, et al., 2003; Montola et al., 2009; Oppermann, 2009) will be reported on in detail. From the 'Seamful Games' experience, Treasure (Bell, 2007) (also known as Bill (Oppermann, 2009; EQUATOR, 2010)) and Feeding Yoshi (Bell, Hall, Chalmers, Gray, & Brown, 2006) were surveyed, but are not reported, because they do not add considerations. Not labeled as a game in Equator, but as a 'Playing and Learning' experience for physical-digital interaction (EQUA-TOR, 2010), Ambient Wood (Thompson et al., 2003; Rogers et al., 2002) is included in the study, because: the project satisfies the inclusion/exclusion criteria; 'playing' can seen as a form of gaming; Ambient Wood is referenced as a pervasive game in de Souza e Silva and Sutko (2009a, p. 255); and, the project adds much to the discussion.

2.2.1.1 CYSMN and URAY

"Citywide [Performance] began with series of exploratory workshops to develop new concepts and technologies" (EQUATOR, 2010), with one of its key technological challenges being to "provide interoperability between heterogeneous devices, such as small mobile devices and collaborative virtual environments" (Izadi et al., 2002). Relevant technologies, created during Citywide were: EQUIP (Equator 'Universal Platform') (Greenhalgh, 2012; Greenhalgh et al., 2001) and later, the EQUIP Component Toolkit (ECT) (Greenhalgh, 2012; Greenhalgh et al., 2004).

Can You See Me Now? is a location-based game where a maximum of fifteen (Steve Benford et al., 2005) online players from the general public, control avatars in a game of chase, through a 3D geo-referenced[2] virtual model of the physical world. Online players move their avatars in an attempt to escape capture from three street runners with a representation in the virtual world. Three performers, playing as street runners, ran through a section of the physical world chasing online players depicted on their game interfaces. Street runners carried mobile devices which: allow their own position to be tracked; showed a 2D map of the area, depicting the online players; and, enabled text-messaging with the online players. In addition, runners carried walkie-talkies, with audio streamed online, to inform online players of the labor involved in the chase and simultaneously enable communication with the control room (Oppermann, 2009). To compensate for GPS inaccuracies, the system was later extended giving street runners more privileged information with regard to online players i.e., street runners were given a map showing GPS coverage and the position of other runners (Crabtree et al., 2004).

---

[2]If virtual coordinates can be exactly transformed into physical coordinates and vice-versa, the result is a virtual world that is a geo-referenced model of the physical world (Oppermann, 2009).

Uncle Roy All Around You also had online players interacting with street players as in CYSMN, but instead of being chased by runners, online players could interact with players 'on the ground' to assist them in, or deter them from, reaching the final goal of finding "an elusive character called Uncle Roy" (Flintham, Anastasi, et al., 2003). The online visual representation was again a 3D virtual representation of the physical world, with players on the ground being directed in a goal oriented manner towards the final destination. Players were monitored through location tracking and direct observation, to ensure safety and that they were on a desired path towards the goal. Characteristic differences from CYSMN were the usage of self-reported positioning (Flintham, Anastasi, et al., 2003; Broll et al., 2006) (instead of GPS, due to inaccuracies (Steve Benford et al., 2004)) and the extensive use of game mastering.

Enabling both CYSMN and URAY was EQUIP, an extensible middleware platform providing a shared data space for the distributed game system, and the ECT, a component designed to deal with the heterogeneity of devices. ECT extends EQUIP to a distributed platform for interconnected components. EQUIP itself is modular and extensible in run-time (Greenhalgh et al. 2001). EQUIP uses pattern matching on items in the data space to route information, making it easy to author a loosely coupled system by changing the data space in run-time (Greenhalgh et al., 2001; Bell, 2007). Although EQUIP does not have a notion of the data types in the data space, various sensor data can be stored and monitored. The extension ECT, allows for the interconnectivity of components, including those responsible for visualization (Greenhalgh et al., 2001, 2004) e.g., collaborative virtual environments.

2.2.1.2 Ambient Wood

Participating children were given goal-oriented motivation to explore a section of woods which had been pre-installed with interactive devices. Children were given a 'probe' device that interacted with the environment via radio waves, light and sound (Thompson et al., 2003). Areas of interest in the woods were demarcated with GPS 'geo-fences' and assigned corresponding areas in a virtual world. Locations of these areas could be altered by reassigning virtual areas to other physical areas, leaving the game intact, but allowing for location adaptability (Thompson et al., 2003). By using a virtual world engine, Ambient Wood attempted to replicate and model the physical world so that "interactions between devices in the physical environment" would have "corresponding interactions within the model". To centrally control interaction, Ambient Wood made use of a virtual world engine called LPMUD. Thompson et al. (2003) were careful to state 'attempted replication' to emphasis the system's dependency on sensed information i.e., sensors with uncertainty in accurately sensing the physical world. Various heterogeneous devices were used in Ambient Wood (e.g., mobile handhelds as sensors or sound actuators), which together formed a distributed system (Thompson et al., 2003). As proxy between the devices and LPMUD, messages were relayed over WLAN through a component called MEAP (MUD-Elvin Application Proxy) (See, 2001; Thompson et al., 2003). The resulting architecture of Ambient Wood, facilitated game mastering, content creation and the alteration of functionality during run-time (Thompson et al., 2003). Operators of installation could intervene and alter the game state, thereby triggering actuators and affecting the physical world.

2.2.2   IPerG

Overlapping with the end of Equator, was an EU funded project called the Integrated Project on Pervasive Gaming (IPerG), which ran between September 2004 and February 2008 (IPerG, 2008). IPerG was said to be producing implementations in the functional areas of: content authoring, game engine development, position services, data persistence, streaming content, orchestration and monitoring, game data analysis and tools to gather user feedback (Ståhl et al., 2007). Almost all of the pervasive games in IPerG satisfy the inclusion/exclusion criteria and were therefore surveyed, but only two are reported. IPerG consists of three 'solutions' consisting of modular technological components, with each solution supporting a number of different pervasive games (IPerG, 2008). To discuss the components in the 'Massively Multiplayer Mobile' (Ståhl et al., 2007) solution, the game called Mythical: The Mobile Awakening (Mythical Mobile) (Holopainen, 2008a, 2008b; Becam et al., 2008; Ståhl et al., 2007) is discussed in detail. To discuss the components from the other two solutions, 'Ubicomp' and 'Augmented Reality', the game called Interference (Waern, Bichard, et al., 2008; Waern, Lindt, et al., 2008) is discussed in detail. Although Momentum (Waern, Lindt, et al., 2008), Day of the Figurines (Flintham, Giannachi, Benford, & Adams, 2007) and Rider Spoke (Oppermann, 2009) were extensive projects, Interference is reported because of its technological diversity.

2.2.2.1   Mythical Mobile

The major theme of Mythical Mobile was for players to control fictive magic, using their mobile devices, against those who aim to disturb the delicate balance of the game world i.e., other players and environmental encounters. The balance of the game world included environmental factors, such as time, weather and moon phases. Players were always virtually present in the game world, even when players were offline (Holopainen, 2008a). Players could track their progress via the web and a scenario editor was included, so that players could build their own content i.e., create their own quests (Holopainen, 2008b). Physical environmental factors could be used as game mechanics, in the player generated content.

To realize Mythical Mobile, several components were combined to form the architecture. The component called Multi-User Publishing Environment (MUPE) was used client-side to support a wide range of mobile devices (Nokia, 2009):

granting access to device hardware (Holopainen, 2008b; Nokia, 2009), providing a rich configurable user interface and communicating with the MUPE server (Ståhl et al., 2007). On the server side, the MUPE server component was combined with EQUIP2 (a rewrite of the original EQUIP (Greenhalgh et al., 2007)) and the Web Application Framework (WAF) (Ståhl et al., 2007), which was comprised of various platform tools (Holopainen, 2008a, 2008b). Although MUPE was originally built to handle an entire game (Suomela, Räsänen, Koivisto, & Mattila, 2004; Becam et al., 2008), MUPE was integrated with EQUIP2 to overcome certain limitations e.g., data persistence (Ståhl et al., 2007); game objects in the MUPE server were stored in the EQUIP2 data space (Becam et al., 2008). The integration of EQUIP2 with the WAF provided support for the development of web applications with direct access to the EQUIP2 data space (Ståhl et al., 2007). The architecture of the WAF allowed for changes to game logic in run-time (Holopainen, 2008a).

2.2.2.2 Interference

In Interference, players were dressed up as technicians and "tasked with repairing the failing Internet and telecoms system in an area" (Waern, Bichard, et al., 2008). Much of the interaction in the game was via devices e.g., a mobile device or one of two custom built devices: a 'Magic Lens' augmented-reality device (a display with virtual content overlaying a real-time video feed) or the music-sensitive doll with various sensors and actuators. Both custom devices were equipped with positioning technology (Waern, Bichard, et al., 2008).

A design goal of Interference was, rapid development by integrating component technologies (Waern, Lindt, et al., 2008). The two middleware components called: Pervasive Interactive Mobile Platform (PIMP) and Pervasive Applications RunTime (PART), allowed for position tracking of the custom doll and mobile phones (Ståhl et al., 2006, 2007; Appelt et al., 2008; Oppermann, 2009). A component called the Morgan VR/AR Framework, allowed for interaction with the Magic Lens device (Ståhl et al., 2007). Linking both PIMP/PART and Morgan was a central component called Game Creator (Waern, Bichard, et al., 2008; Oppermann, 2009). Game Creator could be used to create and manage complex relationships between game objects, with snippets of actions to handle game events (Oppermann, 2009). Because Interference had a distinctive non-technological role-playing part, the game was semi-automatic i.e., mostly automatic, but with parts requiring manual intervention (Waern, Bichard, et al., 2008). Game Creator served as an authoring and game mastering tool for the PIMP/PART and Morgan components (Waern, Bichard, et al., 2008). Although it was reported that Game Creator needed another iteration of development to make it easier to use, the authors concluded that Game Creator and supporting technologies could be a good rapid prototyping tool for pervasive games in general (Oppermann, 2009). Rapid development of Interference was successful, with development spanning only a few months.

To detail the individual technological components: PART is a light-weight middleware designed to provide for the distribution of messages and synchronization of game state (Ståhl et al., 2007); it is a shared data space for devices with an option for data persistence (Ståhl et al., 2006). PIMP supports heterogeneous devices such as sensors, actuators and other components by representing each as an object that can be linked to others (Appelt et al., 2008; Hansson et al., 2007; Ståhl et al., 2007). The Morgan VR/AR Framework was a distributed multi-user framework for virtual worlds. The full version of Morgan was designed as a stand-alone system, including its own graphics renderer and device abstraction layer (DEVAL) (Fraunhofer FIT, 2009; Appelt et al., 2008). However, in IPerG a lighter version of the framework, designed specifically for mobile devices (Appelt et al., 2008), was integrated with PIMP/PART and Game Creator (Ståhl et al., 2007; Waern, Lindt, et al., 2008). Game Creator was an attempt to create a game engine for staging, authoring and game mastering pervasive games (Waern, Bichard, et al., 2008), integrating the PIMP/PART and Morgan components as proof-of-concept. Game Creator supported and handled the complexity for both thick[3] and thin clients. Clients of PIMP/PART being thin clients, utilized the game logic located in Game Creator. Clients of the Morgan VR/AR Framework contained partial game state and were therefore thick clients, requiring some game content to be downloaded from Game Creator prior to play (Waern, Lindt, et al., 2008).

2.2.3   ARQuake

The augmented reality game, ARQuake (Thomas et al., 2000; Oppermann, 2009) is an extension of the original game called Quake (id Software, 1996; Oppermann, 2009), a first-person perspective 3D video game where players fight monsters programmed as autonomous agents i.e., non-player characters (NPCs). The player of ARQuake wore a wearable context-aware computer system; a laptop connected to a head-mounted display, digital compass and two different positioning systems. The system allowed the player to "see not only the [physical] world around them, but also overlaid computer-generated information that enriches the user's perception" (Thomas et al., 2000). ARQuake was built by repurposing the original Quake engine which was already open-source then. In contrast to Ambient Wood, ARQuake was built on a graphics engine rather than a virtual world engine, with a Euclidean spatial representation, that could be directly overlaid onto the physical world. The game area for ARQuake was a limited section of university campus of about 15,000 square meters.

---

[3]Software client, in a client-server typology, heavily loaded with functionality; contrary to a thin client which implements very little functionality, but relies heavily on server computation.

2.2.4   Pac-Man Must Die!

In the game, Pac-Man Must Die! (Sanneblad & Holmquist, 2004; Söderlund, 2009), players play the classic game of Pac-Man, but with a role reversal. Instead of fleeing from ghosts, each player controls a ghost and must flee from Pac-Man. The game plays out on handheld devices configured in a peer-to-peer fashion, with each device constituting a part of a virtual world (Sanneblad & Holmquist, 2004). The game world for Pac-Man Must Die! was distributed across the handheld devices, with the physical orientation of the players and devices playing an important part in the game (Sanneblad & Holmquist, 2004) i.e., dependent on the position of the person holding the device and their willingness to share their view of the game world. The collective virtual world is, what Söderlund (2009) refers to as, a pseudo-persistent world, because it is "created using lots of fragments of a world", where the state of a local world is saved between game sessions, giving the illusion of world persistence when a player visits the same fragment again. Devices communicate in an ad-hoc fashion over WLAN or Bluetooth, with the first mobile device present functioning as server, and the second to join, as a redundant backup server (Sanneblad & Holmquist, 2003). Sanneblad and Holmquist (2004) state support for a broader range of devices as future work.

2.2.5   Team Exploration

The pervasive game called, Team Exploration (Demeure, Gentes, Stuyck, Guyot-Mbodji, & Martin, 2008) was implemented using the Transhumance platform, a software platform devised to run collaborative applications on mobile ad-hoc networks. Team Exploration is similar to Pac-Man Must Die!, but is fully decentralized. Team Exploration was designed as a pervasive collaborative treasure hunt, where: two teams of four players, equipped with mobile WLAN devices, try and find, in a limited time, in which area, depicted on the map, each of four pictures was taken. Team Exploration was explicitly created to demonstrate the Transhumance platform.

2.2.6   STARS

Also in the domain of pervasive gaming, the STARS platform (Magerkurth, Memisoglu, Engelke, & Streitz, 2004) enables a "hybrid class of computer augmented tabletop games". The platform consists of: a touch screen positioned horizontally as game table-top; an overhead camera to track physical game pieces and/or player hands; a large vertical display visible to all players; handheld devices with microphones attached for verbal commands to the STARS system and personal interaction with game; headphones for personal audio output; and, public loudspeakers for ambient audio. Magerkurth et al. (2004) state that several games have been implemented, but that "there is currently no single game to realize all of the potential of STARS".

2.2.7 FinN

Although, positioned as a platform for pervasive games, Akribopoulos et al. (2009) summarize pervasive games as limited to those in a "range from geocaching games, to playing tag-and-chase" (seemingly discounting certain types of pervasive games e.g., augmented table top games, transmedia games or technology-enabled LARP) and targeting mainly those played "in close proximity, most probably indoor environments" and with "rapid physical activity". Although perhaps scoped incorrectly, the Fun in Numbers (FinN) (Akribopoulos et al., 2009; Chatzigiannakis et al., 2011) platform is an important addition to the survey, with respect to combining pervasive games, wireless sensor networks and social media. FinN is a distributed multi-tiered large-scale architecture with four layers: Guardian Layer, Game Station Layer, Game Engine and World Layer. The Guardian Layer is composed of heterogeneous devices and protocols for device discovery. The Guardian Layer communicates with the optional infrastructure 'back-bone' implemented in the Game Station Layer. One station is promoted to Game Engine for each game i.e., the local authority for each physical game site. And lastly, the World Layer is responsible for managing all game instances i.e., the entire system.

2.3 Resulting Component Feature Set

In the previous section, games have been discussed from a cultural perspective, with some introduction to the technologies used. Having gathered all details from the surveyed games, features and underlying issues have been distilled down into the following component feature set, considered central to supporting pervasive games:

- Virtual Game World with World Persistence;
- Shared Data Space(s) with Data Persistence;
- Heterogeneous Devices and Systems;
- Context-Awareness;
- Roles, Groups, Hierarchies, Permissions;
- Current and Historical Game State;
- Game Master Intervention;
- Reconfiguration, Authoring and Scripting in Run-Time;
- and, Bidirectional Diegetic and Non-Diegetic Communication.

In this section, reported games are discussed again, but from a technological perspective relative to the resulting set. One component feature is discussed in each of the following subsections.

2.3.1 Virtual Game World with World Persistence

All reported games made use of virtual game elements (as per the sub-domain criteria) in a spatiotemporal world; game worlds overlapping with the virtual and the physical worlds. In CYSMN, the visualization of the game world for both online and street players was a digital map with moving player positions and scrolling text messages superimposed on upon it. Players interacted with other players through proximity and text messages (Flintham, Steve Benford, et al., 2003). URAY was similar to CYSMN, but with some visualization improvements e.g., online player could switch to a 3D virtual view (Flintham, Steve Benford, et al., 2003). In Ambient Wood, children and objects had a virtual representation in the LPMUD engine, albeit without a visualization. Children interacted with the physical game world, simultaneously interacting and changing the modeled virtual game world (Thompson et al., 2003). The virtual world of Mythical Mobile is similar to that of Ambient Wood, because they both share influence from MUD (Becam et al., 2008; Suomela et al., 2004). Interference made use of Game Creator, where players and objects in the game world had corresponding game objects in the engine (Waern, Lindt, et al., 2008). In ARQuake, the player is in first person perspective interacting with a virtual game world overlaid on the physical world (Thomas et al., 2000). Instead of playing Pac-Man, in the game Pac-Man Must Die!, each players played the role of a different ghost, eating dots in the shared virtual game world, while avoiding Pac-Man (Sanneblad & Holmquist, 2004). Since player proximity to one another mattered, the game world extended into the physical (Söderlund, 2009). Team Exploration is a location-based game geo-referenced to the physical world. STARS supported several games, but players were given control over one or more game pieces in the table-top game; with a subset of pieces having both a virtual and physical presence (Magerkurth et al., 2004). In FinN, player data and game related data was stored locally in the Game Engine layer, synchronizing applicable data with the World Layer (Akribopoulos et al., 2009).

In all of the reported games, virtual game worlds strived to be persistent during times of the staging or during scheduled play times. In CYSMN, players were logged into a seemingly always available world during play times (Flintham, Steve Benford, et al., 2003), but the state of the world was static outside the existence of players i.e., persistency was not sought after (Montola et al., 2009). World persistence in URAY is similar to that of CYSMN. A distinction from CYSMN, being that URAY had game objectives that led from start to finish, limiting game play (and the need for world persistence) to approximately 1 h (Flintham, Anastasi, et al., 2003). Ambient Wood used the LPMUD engine, which fully supported world persistence, but between the 2 h sessions in Ambient Wood, technology was turned off to save battery, restarted and checked before the next session (Rogers et al., 2002). The virtual game world of Mythical Mobile was persistent, with the world continuing, even if players are logged off (Holopainen, 2008a). A game of Interference was 3–5 h long, with game objectives leading from start to finish, similar to that of URAY (Waern, Bichard, et al., 2008). World persistence had to only be maintained for a short period of play time, but Game Creator supported a constantly running game none-the-less (Waern, Lindt, et al., 2008). ARQuake is based on the original Quake, a single player game with the virtual world loaded during the play time (Thomas et al., 2000). World persistence in ARQuake is trivial to simulate, because the world is made available exactly when that single player wants to play. If ARQuake were to be modified to include multiple players, world persistence would be equal to that of STARS (Magerkurth et al., 2004); still simulated with scheduled play times and manual data persistence. Pac-Man Must Die! has been labeled as 'pseudo-persistent', such that fragments of the world are persistent with respect to the player accessing it (Sanneblad & Holmquist, 2004). Team Exploration also supports a pseudo-persistent virtual world, similar to Pac-Man Must Die! "FinN games are meant to be played in every place and at every time" (Akribopoulos et al., 2009), which this author assumes to mean continuously.

2.3.2 Shared Data Space(s) with Data Persistence

Each device or system can maintain one or more data spaces. This means the game state is potentially spread out across an architecture, in many data spaces, with networking being one method to share game state. Network communication between heterogeneous devices and systems requires 'compatibility' (ISO, 2011) when networking. Various communication patterns can be used to coordinate communication between data spaces e.g., EQUIP used a blackboard pattern (Greenhalgh et al., 2001), PIMP and MEAP used a producer/consumer model (Appelt et al., 2008) and the Morgan VR/AR Framework used CORBA (Ståhl et al., 2007). For the decentralized system of Transhumance, to overcome the lack of shared data space, a game can be designed as such that players are enticed to meet at certain locations where a shared game state can be obtained,[4] enabling game mastering or other features.

A centralized architecture means that there is a shared data space where the game state is collected and controlled, with data spaces on devices considered to be volatile or persisted through the centralized system. Devices, when linked to a game engine, frequently play the part of client and do not communicate directly with other devices e.g., as in CYSMN (Greenhalgh et al., 2004), Interference (Waern, Lindt, et al., 2008) and ARQuake (Thomas et al., 2000). All reported games used a

---

[4]It is possible to share game state on a cultural level only e.g., data spaces of the player devices are kept isolated, but players meet to discuss their high scores (Peitz, Saarenpää, & Björk, 2007).

centralized (Armitage, Claypool, & Branch, 2006) architecture, except for Team
Exploration; albeit, in conjunction with perhaps a distributed system of devices
e.g., as in Ambient Wood, Pac-Man Must Die! or FinN. Ambient Wood is a good
example of a centralized data space coordinated by the LPMUD engine, with other
data spaces in the distributed system of sensors and actuators considered volatile.
In Ambient Wood, it is unclear to what extent devices interacted with each other
i.e., possibly forming a decentralized network of clients with one centralized server.
Mobile phones can function as (thin) client or as partial server; the latter if the
mobile phone interacts with other clients and contains game logic and data. Clients
of PIMP/PART (Waern, Lindt, et al., 2008) are a good example of thin clients and
the mobile phones used in Pac-Man Must Die! are a good example of a partial or
full server. Pac-Man Must Die! was implemented as a network of clients, with one
phone dynamically designated as server and one as redundant server (Sanneblad
& Holmquist, 2004). In Team Exploration, the Transhumance platform creates
shared data spaces when nodes of the distributed system meet. Because of the
decentralized nature of Team Exploration, there are possible issues with respect
to security and anti-cheating (Yahyavi & Kemme, 2013). The FinN architecture
supports many games, with a centralized component being optional depending on
the game (Akribopoulos et al., 2009).

For an architecture to be 'fault tolerant' and 'recoverable' (ISO, 2011), data
spaces must have some form of data persistence. In Ambient Wood, LPMUD
handled data persistence in the form of a flat file (Bartle, 2003). The combined
components EQUIP/ECT (Greenhalgh et al., 2004) used in CYSMN and URAY,
and components EQUIP2/WAF/MUPE (Ståhl et al., 2007) used in Mythical Mobile,
integrated with a database for data persistence. Out of the combined components
PIMP/PART, before being used in conjunction with Game Creator in Interference,
it was PART that was responsible for the data space and for data persistence
(through database or flat file) (Ståhl et al., 2006, 2007). In Interference, Game
Creator had direct access to a database for data persistence (Waern, Lindt, et
al., 2008). In the pseudo-persistent world of Pac-Man Must Die!, persistence
was handled by the device that served as redundant backup server (Sanneblad &
Holmquist, 2003). Because of the decentralized nature of the platform, each device
in the Transhumance network was responsible for its own local data persistence. If
ARQuake used the same data persistency as that of Quake, then data persistency
was problematic i.e., persisting and recovering the data space required explicit user
intervention (id Software, 1996), leaving the system vulnerable to system failure.
An explicit lack of data persistence was recognized in STARS (Magerkurth et al.,
2004), and in FinN, the use of a database ensured data persistence (Chatzigiannakis
et al., 2011).

2.3.3   *Heterogeneous Devices and Systems*

Non-standard input devices, comprised of sensors and actuators, form an 'interface' (Nieuwdorp, 2005) between player and the game. In Ambient Wood, many sensors and actuators were carried by the children and also spread out in the physical world (Thompson et al., 2003). As interface to the game, ARQuake utilized a custom built wearable computer system with head-mounted display (Thomas et al., 2000), and in Interference, a music-sensitive doll was built (Waern, Bichard, et al., 2008). Game Creator was designed to separate input/output technologies from the game logic, facilitating rapid adoption of new technologies (Oppermann, 2009). Many heterogeneous devices were used in the STARS platform to interact with the game system e.g., personal displays on handheld devices including microphones for verbal commands (Magerkurth et al., 2004). In CYSMN, URAY, Mythical Mobile, Pac-Man Must Die! and Team Exploration, participants carried mobile devices as a map of the game area (Flintham, Steve Benford, et al., 2003; Flintham, Anastasi, et al., 2003; Ståhl et al., 2007; Demeure et al., 2008), and in Interference, a mobile phone served as custom augmented reality interface (Ståhl et al., 2007; Waern, Lindt, et al., 2008). The wireless sensor network constitutes the devices in the FinN architecture, with the optional Guardian Layer dealing with some of the heterogeneity (Akribopoulos et al., 2009).

To ensure 'interoperability' (ISO, 2011) between heterogeneous devices and systems (e.g., service-oriented architectures), many of the reported systems included a specialized component to function as bridge between data spaces. In the Morgan framework, the component is appropriately named Device Abstraction Layer (DEVAL). DEVAL handled interoperability through a publish/subscribe component using CORBA for network communication (Appelt et al., 2008). The device abstraction layer is a simplification to black box the complexity of interoperability between heterogeneous devices, by abstracting issues into a single component or middleware. Other components acting as device abstraction layers were: ECT (in CYSMN, URAY, and Mythical Mobile), used a tuple-space approach allowing for tuple producers and consumers (Greenhalgh et al., 2004); MEAP (in Ambient Wood), used a publish/subscribe component with bindings for various programming languages (See, 2001); and, PIMP (in Interference), used a producer/consumer model with Bluetooth, TCP and HTTP support (Appelt et al., 2008). In Team Exploration, the Transhumance platform handles interoperability issues and can be considered a device abstraction layer, forming a decentralized distributed system of devices using mobile ad-hoc networking. Magerkurth et al. (2004) speak of a 'device management layer' used in the STARS platform called *RichNet*, but no literature was found pertaining to its implementation.

2.3.4 Context-Awareness

A certain degree of context-awareness (Schilit, Adams, & Want, 1994; Suomela et al., 2004) was universally sought for in all reported games, with CYSMN and ARQuake being explicitly described as context-aware (Suomela et al., 2004). EQUIP/ECT (Greenhalgh et al., 2004) and MUPE (Suomela et al., 2004) technologies were built with context-awareness in mind. Variables taken into account for context-awareness varied greatly e.g., location, body orientation, available resources including network connectivity, proximity to surroundings or noise levels (Schilit et al., 1994). Except for Pac-Man Must Die! (Sanneblad & Holmquist, 2003) and Team Exploration, some form of position localization was required in all reported games, with GPS technology being the most common. Those not using GPS were: URAY, which specifically used self-reported positioning (Flintham, Anastasi, et al., 2003); the STARS platform, which instead used a camera recognition system to track physical objects (Magerkurth et al., 2004); and, the FinN architecture, which uses indoor position localization through its wireless sensor network. Other uses of context-awareness include the need for proximity detection in CYSMN (Flintham, Steve Benford, et al., 2003), Ambient Wood (Thompson et al., 2003) and Team Exploration (called co-presence); and, the detection of body orientation used in ARQuake (Thomas et al., 2000). The optional Guardian Layer in the FinN architecture provides localization and context-awareness through the connected wireless sensor network (Akribopoulos et al., 2009).

Although, sensor enabled heterogeneous devices are a primary source of context information, context information can also be gathered from servers set up as service providers e.g., service-oriented architectures in the form of web services. MUPE allowed for any information on the Internet to be sent to a MUPE application (Suomela et al., 2004), allowing Mythical Mobile to interact with web services to obtain physical environmental data (Holopainen, 2008a). The World Layer in the FinN architecture was responsible for connecting with social media services (Akribopoulos et al., 2009).

One caveat, as a consequence of mobile computing, is that which has been referred to as 'uncertainty' (Steve Benford et al., 2004; Steven Benford et al., 2006; Oppermann, 2009). Uncertainty in position localization and networking was reported as an issue in many of the reported games. Obstacles in the physical world disrupt positioning signals, leading to 'shadow' areas, multiple detection or delays (Oppermann, 2009). Extreme uncertainty in positioning leads to erratic readings or loss of tracking. In CYSMN, tracking proved so problematic that the street runners themselves needed to compensate for the margins of error. And, in the later production, URAY, self-reported positioning was opted for instead of position tracking (Oppermann, 2009; Steven Benford et al., 2006; Flintham, Anastasi, et al., 2003). In STARS, readings from the camera recognition system produced uncertainty due to being misaligned with the physical world (Magerkurth et al., 2004). Similar disruption is applicable to network connectivity, with extreme network uncertainty leading to a disconnected state (Appelt et al., 2008; Broll et al., 2006).

Network connectivity was an issue in both CYSMN (Flintham, Steve Benford, et al., 2003; Crabtree et al., 2004), and Ambient Wood (Thompson et al., 2003). Transhumance supports a chat service that is tolerant to disconnections; if a player is out of reach messages are exchanged the next time the two devices reconnect. The use of 'delay-tolerant' network communication is used to compensate for network uncertainty, in the FinN architecture (Akribopoulos et al., 2009; Chatzigiannakis et al., 2011).

2.3.5 Roles, Groups, Hierarchies, Permissions

The puppet master is example of a game master, pulling strings behind the scenes, but other roles are possible. In CYSMN, street runners are not just players, but performers (NPCs) with a role in staging the game (Crabtree et al., 2004). Street runners were given extra privileged information in comparison to online players e.g., GPS/WLAN coverage and the locations of other runners (Crabtree et al., 2004). Crabtree et al. (2004) describe game mastering in CYSMN as decentralized i.e., a collection of perspectives from different game masters 'on the ground', instead of in a centralized control room. Roles were even more prevalent in URAY, with at least three distinguishable: performers with a diegetic role interacting with the player, performers in an operations role assisting the player and puppet masters (Flintham, Anastasi, et al., 2003). To emphasize each role in URAY, interfaces to the game differed for each role (Flintham, Anastasi, et al., 2003). It is possible to enroll players temporarily into a game mastering function; this was the case in Mythical Mobile, where the player that created the quest for other players served as game master (Holopainen, 2008a). In Interference, seven players were each given a distinct role, each with different equipment; one game master was used and three actors (Waern, Bichard, et al., 2008). Roles used in Interference were supported by Game Creator (Waern, Lindt, et al., 2008).

Roles can be organized in groups, such as the group of street runners in CYSMN, or in a hierarchy, such as the underlying structure found in LPMUD, that Ambient Wood is built upon (Thompson et al., 2003). Each role or group can be assigned different permissions to access or actuate the game state. Restricting permission can be achieved through a role specific interface with limited access (e.g., CYSMN (Crabtree et al., 2004)) or by limiting access to parts of the game state through control structures (e.g., Ambient Wood). The MEAP component, in Ambient Wood, was given a privileged 'wizard' role found in LPMUD with permissions to be able to make updates to the game state, namely to change the virtual positions of players (Thompson et al., 2003). Transhumance supports groups with a 'security system' dictating player permissions.

2.3.6   Current and Historical Game State

The game state, of each of the reported games, included various amounts of player information. In CYSMN and URAY, background details of the street players included name, gender and appearance, accompanied by a photograph (Flintham, Anastasi, et al., 2003); in Mythical Mobile, players were allowed to chose an identifier (Holopainen, 2008a); and, in Pac-Man Must Die!, players were recognized by the identifier of the device used (Sanneblad & Holmquist, 2004). In the FinN architecture, player information was synchronized between the Game Engine and World Layer (Akribopoulos et al., 2009).

To monitor the progress of the game in run-time, various technologies provided a view of the current internal game state. Interfaces in CYSMN provided privileged information to street runners (Crabtree et al., 2004). In URAY, game masters tracked "last reported player positions" and the 'technical status' of players through specialized management interfaces (Flintham, Anastasi, et al., 2003). ECT, which was used in both CYSMN and URAY, was built with "emphasis on inspectable properties" (Greenhalgh et al., 2004). The WAF, used in Mythical Mobile, allowed for players, serving as game master, to view the current game state (Holopainen, 2008a) held in the EQUIP2 data space (Ståhl et al., 2007; Appelt et al., 2008). To view the PART data space, a specialized browser component was built (Ståhl et al., 2007). And, Game Creator, which was built as a GM interface, provided direct access to the game state (Jonsson & Waern, 2008).

To obtain a historical perspective of the game state, the logging of event data was used in many of the technologies. The Equator games CYSMN (Steven Benford et al., 2006), URAY (Flintham, Anastasi, et al., 2003; Steve Benford et al., 2004) and Ambient Wood (Thompson et al., 2003) used logging enabled through ECT (Greenhalgh et al., 2004). In IPerG, logging of events was a later addition (Ståhl et al., 2007), enabled through technologies PIMP (Hansson et al., 2007), PART (Ståhl et al., 2007), the WAF (Appelt et al., 2008) and Game Creator (Waern, Lindt, et al., 2008; Jonsson & Waern, 2008). STARS mentions the recording of game events and histories as future work (Magerkurth et al., 2004). A historical perspective was used for post-game analysis in: CYSMN (Steve Benford et al., 2004); URAY (Steve Benford et al., 2004); Ambient Wood (Rogers et al., 2002); Mythical Mobile through the WAF (Appelt et al., 2008); and, Interference through PART and a specialized log analysis tool (Ståhl et al., 2007). In Ambient Wood, analysis was needed particularly post-game, because of the distributed system; not all device logs were relayed back to the game engine and so had to be collected, assembled and analyzed after the fact (Thompson et al., 2003). Transhumance supports current and historical game state per device only.

On a meta-level (strictly non-diegetic) pertaining to the game state, Game Creator allows for "game masters to make arbitrary notes about players and game objects, [but] the system does not maintain historic information about such notes" (Jonsson & Waern, 2008).

2.3.7   Game Master Intervention

To run a game semi-automatic, rather than fully automatic, game master intervention is needed. In URAY (Flintham, Anastasi, et al., 2003) and Ambient
Wood (Thompson et al., 2003), game masters intervened in the game by directly
manipulating the internal game state. The combined technologies PIMP/PART
featured properties on game objects that could be manipulated in run-time (Ståhl
et al., 2007) i.e., the game state manipulated directly (Hansson et al., 2007).
Specialized interfaces or GM tools, aid game masters in: monitoring the game,
intervening in run-time and manipulating the game state, potentially translating
massive amounts collected game data into a human consumable form. In IPerG,
which had a large focus on game mastering, the predominant strategy for building
GM tools and interfaces was to use web-based solutions. The WAF was integrated
with EQUIP2 and MUPE allowed for HTML/browser based interactions to be
used in Mythical Mobile (Ståhl et al., 2007; Holopainen, 2008a; Appelt et al.,
2008). Property changes in Interference were facilitated by the authoring tool, Game
Creator (Waern, Lindt, et al., 2008; Jonsson & Waern, 2008), allowing functionality
to be manually controlled by the game master (Waern, Bichard, et al., 2008). Game
Creator offered an external interface that allowed it to function as a service-oriented
architecture. And, Waern, Bichard, et al. (2008) state Interference to be the "first
game in IPerG that implements a complete and yet semi-automatic game engine".
Transhumance supports game master intervention through communication only, and
game mastering is problematic because it is difficult to technically monitor all nodes
in a decentralized distributed system. In the FinN architecture, the World Layer can
be used to manage the entire system (Akribopoulos et al., 2009), but no use of
game mastering or orchestration was mentioned. The Game Engine engine featured
an 'embedded Web container', but it was only mentioned as being used to provide
players additional information (Akribopoulos et al., 2009). It is assumed that feature
could be easily extended to support a game master interface.

2.3.8   Reconfiguration, Authoring and Scripting in Run-Time

Pre-game, before a pervasive game is ready to be run, the architecture might still
need to be reconfigured, content authored or the rules altered, so as to adapt the
game to the context of the staging. Pre-game authoring and reconfiguration was
used in Ambient Wood (Thompson et al., 2003) and Interference (Waern, Bichard,
et al., 2008) for location adaptability. Reconfiguration, authoring and scripting
can extend into the in-game phase. Reconfiguration involves changing data-driven
settings in software, hardware and devices; possibly through a GM interface. In the
games CYSMN and URAY, reconfiguration was made possible in run-time by the
combined components EQUIP/ECT e.g., through direct access to the data space and
'extensibility' through the loading of code in run-time (Greenhalgh et al., 2004).

In Ambient Wood, game masters could use the LPMUD text-based interface to access the game engine configuration, changing the virtual model and its effects on the physical world (Thompson et al., 2003). PIMP was designed to "open up the game system for user creation and configuration [...] supporting rapid and simple reconfigurability" (Appelt et al., 2008).

To have a dynamic story and content, game masters might want to author content throughout the in-game phase. In Ambient Wood, new content could be created in run-time (Thompson et al., 2003). The successor to EQUIP, EQUIP2, was combined with MUPE and the WAF (Ståhl et al., 2007), and explicitly used in Mythical Mobile with "user created content in mind" (Becam et al., 2008) e.g., players authored campaigns, encounters and events for other players (Becam et al., 2008; Holopainen, 2008a). The WAF supported web-based authoring tools and MUPE supported a dynamic user interface (Ståhl et al., 2007). In Interference, PART and Game Creator were used for authoring (Waern, Bichard, et al., 2008), allowing for content to be added in run-time (Waern, Lindt, et al., 2008).

To provide functionality to content and change the rules of the game, a scripting language can be used. Script languages are generally either data-definition or run-time languages (Gregory, 2009). Data-definition languages allow a data structure to be populated and read by the engine, while run-time languages are executed by the engine during run-time. ECT was explicitly built to support a run-time scripting language (Greenhalgh et al., 2004; EQUATOR, 2006). In Ambient Wood, the existing run-time scripting language in LPMUD, was used to adapt functionality in run-time (Thompson et al., 2003). Mythical Mobile made use of both data-definition and run-time languages; the EQUIP2 data space used data-definition languages to adapt the game content, while run-time scripts were sent from the server-side to the client, to control the user interface (Becam et al., 2008; Suomela et al., 2004). Game Creator used a data-definition language in the form of predefined snippets of actions (Oppermann, 2009; Waern, Lindt, et al., 2008). Given a scripting language that is sufficiently rich, it is possible to code autonomous NPCs with varying degrees of capabilities. In Mythical Mobile, automated NPCs were created by assigning them a number of predefined functional characteristics i.e., recombinations of existing functionality (Becam et al., 2008). ARQuake, like it's predecessor Quake, implemented their 'autonomous agent' behavior in a run-time scripting language called 'QuakeC' (id Software, 1996; Thomas et al., 2000). Although Magerkurth et al. (2004) stated that "there is room for both human and AI [automated] controlled NPCs even in the same game", the STARS platform didn't support autonomous NPCs. The clarification for this being that autonomous NPCs "pale against the richness of the social interaction with a human game master" e.g., the coded behavior thereof could not be altered during play (Magerkurth et al., 2004).

An environment that can be reconfigured, authored and scripted, might be sufficiently powerful to support simulation. If game events can be simulated, this opens up the possibility for using the 'Wizard of Oz' (WOz) technique (Dow et al., 2005) for testing the architecture pre-game or compensate for system failure in-game (Ståhl et al., 2007). Three technologies mention support for the WOz technique: the WAF, used in a production previous to Mythical Mobile

(Appelt et al., 2008); LPMUD, used in Ambient Wood (Thompson et al., 2003; Rogers et al., 2002); and, Game Creator, used in Interference (Jonsson & Waern, 2008). Transhumance does not mention support for reconfiguration, authoring or scripting in runtime.

2.3.9   Bidirectional Diegetic and Non-diegetic Communication

To communicate the actuated game state to the players, much of the reported games relied on player interfaces to convey alterations e.g., changes in the game state of the LPMUD engine of Ambient Wood would affect the behavior of the heterogeneous devices in the woods (Thompson et al., 2003). Communication through a player interface is a diegetic channel. In URAY, a bi-directional chat and short audio clips (7 s) (Flintham, Anastasi, et al., 2003), from street player to the online player, could be used for both non- and diegetic communication. Having a player meet an NPC in-game (Flintham, Anastasi, et al., 2003), in URAY, is bi-directional diegetic communication (unless the NPC breaks character). Adult facilitators in Ambient Wood, carried walkie-talkies as a non-diegetic bidirectional channel, with the children being monitored through unidirectional microphones (Rogers et al., 2002). In Interference, players where in constant diegetic bi-directional communication with two in-game characters via mobile phone (Waern, Bichard, et al., 2008). In the STARS platform, headsets with microphone and ear speakers provide a diegetic bi-directional channel with the game engine. And, mobile devices allowed each player to have a private conversation with other players in the form of messages (Magerkurth et al., 2004). The games CYSMN (Crabtree et al., 2004), URAY (Flintham, Anastasi, et al., 2003) and Ambient Wood (Rogers et al., 2002) all used walkie-talkies as a non-diegetic communication channel for game mastering. Transhumance implements different chat channels for either non- or diegetic communication, but only with players in proximity.

2.4   Related Work

While searching for pervasive games/projects and technologies, various related work was uncovered. A general overview of related work is provided in the following section (Sect. 2.4.1), followed by a discussion of related work per component, in Sect. 2.4.2.

2.4.1 Other Surveys and Architectures

In a similar survey by Broll et al. (2006) important technologies for augmented-reality pervasive games have been summarized. Broll et al. (2006) mention the development of a pervasive game engine as 'the logical next step', but, unfortunately, do not discuss the details of what constitutes a pervasive game engine e.g., in relation to concepts such as persistence, interoperability, game mastering and communication. All features mentioned in Broll et al. (2006) are also covered herein, albeit organized to highlight the importance of ubiquitous computing in pervasive games, rather than on crossmedia augmentation for augmented-reality games. Some issues found in the survey herein are also mentioned by Broll et al. (2006) in passing, but how those issues affect the game architecture is not discussed e.g., issues of interoperability, mobile networking and (non-)diegetic communication are summarized under the category of 'communication', rather than being worked out in detail. Issues from their survey that overlap with issues of the survey herein are discussed in the next section (Sect. 2.4.2).

Kasapakis, Gavalas, and Bubaris (2013) have surveyed the 'state of the art' in pervasive games, studying ten pervasive games according to several design aspects. Although significantly smaller, their survey touches upon almost all the features mentioned in the survey herein. Less detail is given on features such as a persistent virtual world, context-awareness and orchestration, and how those features impact the game architecture.

Several frameworks and middleware have already been suggested for pervasive games (Papakonstantinou & Brujic-Okretic, 2009; Trinta, Ferraz, & Ramalho, 2006; Lim, Nijdam, & Magnenat-Thalmann, 2008). The comparison of these frameworks and middleware with existing engines on a per-component basis is left for another publication.

2.4.2 Relative to Each Component Feature

Rather than handle the related work intermittently while discussing the component feature set in Sect. 2.3, this section discusses related work per component of the feature set, one section per component.

2.4.2.1 Virtual Game World with World Persistence

In relation to virtual game worlds with world persistence, Montola et al. (2009, p. 65), state that "many pervasive games feature persistent virtual worlds", but not all. Branton et al. (2011) state that "pervasive games require a digital environment that is always available". Greenhalgh et al. (2001), makers of EQUIP, state that combining the physical and the virtual to support ubiquitous computing, allows for the "ability to exploit the coextensive virtual world as a 'behind the scenes' resource for coordinating and managing devices and interaction in the physical space". And, Broll et al. (2006) explain that a game engine (to sustain the world) should be robust and fault tolerant i.e., 'reliable' (ISO, 2011). To maintain a persistent world, the architectures mentioned must support 'reliability' (ISO, 2011) i.e., 'mature' systems, preventing failure by being 'fault tolerant' and supporting 'recoverability'. To be able to offload the world when not active, but to be loaded again later, an architecture must support data persistence.

2.4.2.2   Shared Data Space(s) with Data Persistence

Caltagirone, Keys, Schlief, and Willshire (2002) declare that it is easier to build a game engine using a centralized architecture, to ensure 'security' (ISO, 2011) and prevent 'cheating' (Armitage et al., 2006). Such a centralized architecture allows the shared data space to be protected (Yahyavi & Kemme, 2013). In corroboration of persistent data, Paelke, Oppermann, and Reimann (2008) state that "persistent data-storage for all assets (including the log-files) remains a key issue" for mobile location-based gaming.

2.4.2.3   Heterogeneous Devices and Systems

Branton et al. (2011) state that the number of heterogeneous devices that can be used in pervasive games is increasing. Broll et al. (2006) have identified three different categories of input/output devices that are used in 'crossmedia' games: personal, public and environmental. Sensors for personal or public (more than one participant) data, beyond input/output interaction was not mentioned. Sensors for environmental data was mentioned e.g., instrumenting temperature, wind direction and velocity. Montola et al. (2009, p. 168) identify four strategies for 'giving technology a role in a game', namely as a: gaming device, diegetic artifact, body extension or as technology embedded in the environment.

2.4.2.4   Context-Awareness

Player position is a form of context-awareness; the localization thereof mentioned by Broll et al. (2006) as a "challenge for almost all types of pervasive games". Uncertainty both in position localization and networking is documented in literature (Oppermann, 2009; Branton et al., 2011) e.g., work on coping with uncertainty (Steven Benford et al., 2006), inaccuracies in measurement due to uncertainty (Dow et al., 2005), and disconnectivity (Broll et al., 2006; Paelke et al., 2008). Broll et al. (2006) mention a distinction between pervasive games and other multiplayer games, in that "players in pervasive games may leave the game without sending any notification", and that in some pervasive games, it is possible for a player to make game related actions while offline. In order to effectively game master, Jonsson, Waern, Montola, and Stenros (2007) state that a pervasive game needs a sensory system. And, according to Montola et al. (2009, p. 185), mobile phones can serve as a 'context sensory platform'. The association between context-awareness and pervasive games can be readily found in literature (Steve Benford et al., 2004; Bell, 2007; Branton et al., 2011). To provide geographical context information in location-based games, Paelke et al. (2008) show the relevance of map data (provided by GIS) on different levels of a game architecture. And, Rashid, Mullins, Coulton, and Edwards (2006) mention a number of different map data implementations that can be used.

2.4.2.5 Roles, Groups, Hierarchies, Permissions

The game master role of puppet master has been mentioned in the background on staging in Sect. 1.6. Oppermann (2009) and Koleva et al. (2001) corroborate the use of actors as a role in pervasive games. Jonsson et al. (2007) describe the existence of an "intermediary role between the fully immersed participants and the game masters". Bell (2007) connects the use of roles in pervasive games to research on systems for cooperative work, citing that "a lack of support for flexible roles can be detrimental in CSCW [computer-supported cooperative work]" and that by "maintaining a consistent interface for different roles it is easier for users to assume new roles". The need for grouping players in teams is corroborated by Broll et al. (2006).

2.4.2.6 Current and Historical Game State

Jonsson et al. (2007) state that player and character information is part of the game state that must be considered during game mastering. Broll et al. (2006) and Jonsson et al. (2007) state that player information can include: name, photo and contact information. Game masters need a way to view and modify the current game state (Broll et al., 2006; Jonsson & Waern, 2008). Broll et al. (2006) corroborate that "game orchestration is a major issue in pervasive games" and that "supporting game orchestration and surveillance requires an appropriate support tool". "In order to support decision making, the game master system must be able to provide the game master with both an overview of the current state of the game, as well as maintain historic information about the game and allow the game masters to navigate this history" (Jonsson & Waern, 2008). Broll et al. (2006) implemented a logging tool to support "an in-depth evaluation of the game play, allowing for playback [of] a gaming session in combination with the orchestration tool".

2.4.2.7 Game Master Intervention

In their mixed reality production called Desert Rain, Koleva et al. (2001) state that game master intervention should be possible, if necessary, but "with minimal disruption to their [player] engagement".

2.4.2.8 Reconfiguration, Authoring and Scripting in Run-Time

Broll et al. (2006) recognize the need for pre-game preparation, including reconfiguration of the game to the location of the staging and initialization of the game state. Besides an orchestration tool, Broll et al. (2006) mention the usefulness of an authoring tool that "eases the creation of content and the game logic". Paelke et al. (2008) similarly note the importance of authoring tools in mobile location-based games. Because Jonsson et al. (2007) state that "game mastering can also include active authoring of content to fit the activities of the participants", it would seem to indicate that game mastering and authoring tools could be one and the same, aside from the consideration of which role the tool caters to and the permissions needed to withhold privileged information. Not mentioning scripting per say, but Jonsson and Waern (2008) state that "on occasion the game masters would even reprogram the rules of the game in run time". And, in corroboration of simulation for the WOz technique, Broll et al. (2006) state that the game engine "does not have to care whether the input is from a real sensor or whether this is just a simulator" and that "in order to allow easy and independent testing, it [the game engine] should not distinguish between real and virtual items and I/O [input/output]" i.e., enabling the WOz technique.

2.4.2.9 Bidirectional Diegetic and Non-diegetic Communication

In game mastering, Jonsson and Waern (2008) stress the importance for a game master system to "push information to the players" and that game masters can push "in-game as well as meta-level information to players" i.e., diegetic and non-diegetic information. Some of this communication can be achieved via user interface elements (Jonsson et al., 2007; Koleva et al., 2001). To effectively game master Dessert Rain, authors Koleva et al. (2001) identified three styles of intervention: off-face, virtual and face-to-face interventions. Off-face interventions "cannot be conducted without the players noticing them. But [their] performers [...] always manage to embed the intervention within the game" i.e., a form diegetic unidirectional communication. Players were encouraged to help each other, extending this style of intervention to bi-directional. Virtual interventions were designed to be completely diegetic, "carefully conducted so that the players do not notice them". Face-to-face intervention was used as a last resort and "always results in an interruption of the player's engagement in the game" i.e., an example of non-diegetic bi-directional communication. Broll et al. (2006) mention the use of speech communication in all prototypes, but do not distinguish if they are diegetic or not.

2.5 Discussion and Verification

To summarize the contribution of projects in the survey: Equator contributes primarily with research pertaining to heterogeneous devices and the interoperability thereof, with some focus on game mastering; IPerG contributes heavily with game mastering and pervasive technologies; ARQuake contributes as a single player, pervasive video game; Pac-Man Must Die! and Team Explorer contribute as, centralized and decentralized pseudo-persistent worlds based on an ad-hoc distributed system; STARS as a non-mobile pervasive gaming platform; and FinN with its connectivity to wireless sensor networks and service-oriented architectures, in the form of social media.

In order to verify the distilled feature set, the set needs to be verified against the definitions of pervasive games, summarized in Sect. 1.5. Here, it is shown how the feature set can be used to derive the concept of ubiquitous computing and then differentiated into concept of pervasive games.

2.5.1 Feature Set to Ubiquitous Computing

A *virtual game world with world persistence* (Sect. 2.3.1) that has a *shared data space with data persistence* (Sect. 2.3.2), through a reliable architecture, can be equated to a persistent virtual world. A pervasive game is one where the game world is persistent in the physical world (Montola et al., 2009; Nieuwdorp, 2007) and it is precisely through temporal expansion that pervasive games share the trait of persistence with virtual worlds (de Souza e Silva & Sutko, 2009b) (as per Sect. 1.4). If a pervasive game makes use of a virtual game world, then persistence of that world must at least be simulated. If an engine is to be able to stage a broad range of pervasive games, then the engine must provide for 'ubiquitous availability' (Dionisio, Burns III, & Gilbert, 2013) to the persistent virtual world. In addition to availability and in order to support a broad range of games, the game architecture must also provide for 'ubiquity of access' (Schilit et al., 1994; Dionisio et al., 2013) to the persistent virtual world through *heterogeneous devices and systems* (Sect. 2.3.3). A device abstraction layer ensures interoperability and links the devices and systems to *shared data space(s)* (Sect. 2.3.2). Heterogeneous devices, qualifying as non-standard input and output devices (Nieuwdorp, 2007), providing *context-awareness* (Sect. 2.3.4) as a sensory system that pervades into the background. Additional context information can be obtained from heterogeneous systems that provide services. Ubiquitous availability and access, heterogeneous technologies and context-awareness together provide for the ubiquity or pervasiveness in pervasive games (Nieuwdorp, 2007; Dionisio et al., 2013; Abowd, 1999).

2.5.2 Ubiquitous Computing to Pervasive Games

To differentiate pervasive games from pervasive or ubiquitous computing, the gaming aspect of pervasive games needs to be accounted for. Of course, the engine itself should allow the actual game to be created e.g., including any goals, conflicts and outcomes of the game (Adams & Rollings, 2006; Montola, 2012). One distinction from pervasive computing lies in relation to ubiquity of access; pervasive computing without access to a computing device might prove difficult, but a player partially denied access to a computing devices can potentially still be in the game. To describe not just a game, but a pervasive game, a pervasive game engine must be prepared to handle spatial, temporal and social expansion (Montola, 2012). A persistent virtual world mapped to the physical world, through heterogeneous devices, provides for: spatial expansion through a blending with the physical world and temporal expansion through ubiquitous availability. *Reconfiguration, content authoring and scripting in run-time* (Sect. 2.3.8), allows for a pervasive game to be adapted to the context of the staging, pervading the game further into the physical and catering to the participants. To handle social expansion, it should be possible to assign players, NPCs and game masters different *roles*, organize them into *groups and hierarchies* (Sect. 2.3.5), each with a different set of access and actuation *permissions*. *Game master intervention* (Sect. 2.3.7) is required so that game masters can access and actuate the *current and historical game state* (Sect. 2.3.6). And, lastly, social expansion is supported by participants communicating through *bi-directional diegetic and non-diegetic communication* (Sect. 2.3.9) channels.

References

Abowd, G. D. (1999, May). Software engineering issues for ubiquitous computing. In *Proceedings of the 1999 international conference on software engineering* (pp. 75–84). Los Angeles, CA, USA: IEEE.

Adams, E., & Rollings, A. (2006). *Fundamentals of game design (game design and development series)*. Upper Saddle River, NJ, USA: Prentice-Hall, Inc.

Akribopoulos, O., Logaras, M., Vasilakis, N., Kokkinos, P., Mylonas, G., Chatzigiannakis, I., & Spirakis, P. (2009). Developing multiplayer pervasive games and networked interactive installations using ad hoc mobile sensor nets. In *Proceedings of the international conference on advances in computer enterntainment technology* (pp. 174–181). New York, NY, USA: ACM.

Ampatzoglou, A., & Stamelos, I. (2010, May). Software engineering research for computer games: a systematic review. *Information and Software Technology, 52* (9), 888–901.

Appelt, W., Ohlenburg, J., Greenhalgh, C., Oppermann, L., & Åkesson, K.-P. (2008, April). *Deliverable D7.7: final software delivery of WP 7.*

Armitage, G., Claypool, M., & Branch, P. (2006). *Networking and online games, understanding and engineering multiplayer internet games.* Chichester, West Sussex, England: John Wiley & Sons, Ltd.

Bartle, R. (2003). *Designing virtual worlds.* Indianapolis, Indiana, USA: New Riders Publishing.

Becam, A., Milding, R., Nenonen, V., Nummenmaa, T., & Kuittinen, J. (2008, March). *Deliverable D13.6 appendix B: Mythical, the mobile awakening technical report.*

Bell, M. (2007). *Guidelines and infrastructure for the design and implementation of highly adaptive, context-aware, mobile, peer-to-peer systems.* (Doctoral dissertation, University of Glasgow, Faculty of Information and Mathematical Sciences, Department of Computing Science).

Bell, M., Hall, M., Chalmers, M., Gray, P., & Brown, B. (2006, May). Domino: exploring mobile collaborative software adaptation. In *Pervasive computing* (Vol. 3968, pp. 153–168). Lecture Notes in Computer Science. Dublin, Ireland: Springer Berlin Heidelberg.

Benford, S., Magerkurth, C., & Ljungstrand, P. (2005). Bridging the physical and digital in pervasive gaming. *Communications of the ACM, 48* (3), 54–57.

Benford, S., Seager, W., Flintham, M., Anastasi, R., Rowland, D., Humble, J., … Sutton, J. (2004). The error of our ways: the experience of self- reported position in a location-based game. In *Ubiquitous computing* (pp. 70–87). UbiComp 2004. Nottingham, UK: Springer Berlin Heidelberg.

Benford, S., Crabtree, A., Flintham, M., Drozd, A., Anastasi, R., Paxton, M., … Row-Farr, J. (2006, March). Can You See Me Now? *ACM Transactions on Computer-Human Interaction (TOCHI), 13* (1), 100–133.

Branton, C., Carver, D., & Ullmer, B. (2011). Interoperability standards for pervasive games. In *Proceedings of the 1st international workshop on games and software engineering* (pp. 40–43). New York, NY, USA: ACM.

Broll, W., Ohlenburg, J., Lindt, I., Herbst, I., & Braun, A.-K. (2006, October). Meeting technology challenges of pervasive augmented reality games. In *Proceedings of 5th ACM SIGCOMM workshop on network and system support for games* (p. 28). Singapore: ACM.

Caltagirone, S., Keys, M., Schlief, B., & Willshire, M. J. (2002). Architecture for a massively multiplayer online role playing game engine. *Journal of Computing Sciences in Colleges, 18* (2), 105–116.

Chatzigiannakis, I., Mylonas, G., Kokkinos, P., Akribopoulos, O., Logaras, M., & Mavrommati, I. (2011). Implementing multiplayer pervasive installations based on mobile sensing devices: field experience and user evaluation from a public showcase. *Journal of Systems and Software, 84* (11), 1989–2004.

Crabtree, A., Benford, S., Rodden, T., Greenhalgh, C., Flintham, M., Anastasi, R., … Steed, A. (2004). Orchestrating a mixed reality game 'on the ground'. In *Proceedings of the SIGCHI conference on human factors in computing systems* (pp. 391–398). CHI '04. Vienna, Austria: ACM.

de Souza e Silva, A., & Sutko, D. M. (Eds.). (2009a). *Digital cityscapes.* USA: Peter Lang.

de Souza e Silva, A., & Sutko, D. M. (2009b). Digital cityscapes. (Chap. Merging Digital and Urban Playspaces: An introduction to the Field, pp. 1–20). USA: Peter Lang.

Demeure, I., Gentes, A., Stuyck, J., Guyot-Mbodji, A., & Martin, L. (2008). Transhumance: a platform on a mobile ad hoc network challenging collaborative gaming. In *Collaborative technologies and systems, 2008. CTS 2008. international symposium on* (pp. 221–228). Irvine, CA, USA: IEEE.

Dionisio, J. D., Burns III, W. G., & Gilbert, R. (2013). 3D virtual worlds and the metaverse: current status and future possibilities. *ACM Computing Surveys, 45* (3), 34:1–34:38.

Dow, S., Lee, J., Oezbek, C., MacIntyre, B., Bolter, J. D., & Gandy, M. (2005). Wizard of oz interfaces for mixed reality applications. In *CHI '05 extended abstracts on human factors in computing systems* (pp. 1339–1342). New York, NY, USA: ACM.

EQUATOR. (2006). *EQUIP and the EQUATOR component toolkit (ECT) homepage.* Retrieved from http://equip.sourceforge.net/

EQUATOR. (2010, September). *EQUATOR Interdisciplinary Research Collaboration (IRC).* Retrieved from http://web.archive.org/web/20100914131736/http://www.equator.ac.uk

Flintham, M., Anastasi, R., Benford, S., Drozd, A., Mathrick, J., Rowland, D., . . . Sutton, J. (2003, November). Uncle roy all around you: mixing games and theatre on the city streets. In *Level up conference proceedings.* University of Utrecht: DiGRA.

Flintham, M., Benford, S., Anastasi, R., Hemmings, T., Crabtree, A., Greenhalgh, C., . . . Row-Farr, J. (2003, April). Where on-line meets on the streets: experiences with mobile mixed reality games. In *Proceedings of the SIGCHI conference on human factors in computing systems* (pp. 569–576). CHI '03. New York, NY, USA: ACM.

Flintham, M., Giannachi, G., Benford, S., & Adams, M. (2007, June). Day of the figurines: a slow narrative-driven game for mobile phones using text messaging. In *4th international symposium on pervasive gaming applications (PerGames)* (pp. 167–175). ICVS'07. Salzburg, Austria: Springer-Verlag.

Fraunhofer FIT. (2009, July). *Morgan - a distributed multi-user framework for VR/AR applications.* Retrieved from https://web.archive.org/web/20100530045127/http://fit.fraunhofer.de/morgan

Freeman, R. (2004, September). *Mixed reality toolkit, MSc VIVE final year project report.*

Greenhalgh, C. (2012). *Chris Greenhalgh's home page.* Retrieved from http://www.crg.cs.nott.ac.uk/~cmg/

Greenhalgh, C., Benford, S., Drozd, A., Flintham, M., Hampshire, A., Oppermann, L., . . . von Tycowicz, C. (2007). Concepts and technologies for pervasive games, a reader for pervasive gaming research vol. 1. (Chap. EQUIP2: A Platform for Mobile Phone-based Game Development, Vol. 1, pp. 147–172). Shaker Verlag GmbH.

Greenhalgh, C., Izadi, S., Mathrick, J., Humble, J., & Taylor, I. (2004, September). ECT: a toolkit to support rapid construction of ubicomp environments. In *Proceedings of workshop on system support for ubiquitous computing.* UbiSys. Nottingham, UK: Springer Verlag.

Greenhalgh, C., Izadi, S., Rodden, T., & Benford, S. (2001). *The EQUIP platform: bringing together physical and virtual worlds.*

Gregory, J. (2009, July). *Game engine architecture* (J. Lander & M. Whiting, Eds.). Wellesley, Massachusetts: A K Peters.

Hanke, J., & Geiger, P. (2015, January). *Reality as a virtual playground.* Retrieved from http://www.makinggames.biz/features/reality-as-a-virtual-playground,7286.html

Hansson, P., Åkesson, K.-P., & Wallberg, A. (2007, February). *Deliverable D11.9: second generation core platform.*

Holopainen, J. (2008a, March). *Deliverable D13.6 appendix a: game design document – mythical: the mobile awakening.*

Holopainen, J. (2008b, March). *Deliverable D13.6: final report: massively multiplayer mobile.*

id Software. (1996). Quake.

IPerG. (2008). *IPerG (integrated project on pervasive gaming) consortium.* Retrieved from http://iperg.sics.se

ISO. (2011). *ISO/IEC 25010:2011 systems and software engineering – systems and software quality requirements and evaluation (SQuaRE) – system and software quality models.*

Izadi, S., Fraser, M., Benford, S., Flintham, M., Greenhalgh, C., Rodden, T., & Schnädelbach, H. (2002, January). Citywide: supporting interactive digital experiences across physical space. *Personal and Ubiquitous Computing, 6* (4), 290–298.

Johannesson, P., & Perjons, E. (2014). *An introduction to design science.* Springer International Publishing Switzerland.

Jonsson, S., & Waern, A. (2008). Art of game-mastering pervasive games, the. In *Proceedings of the 2008 international conference on advances in computer entertainment technology* (pp. 224–231). ACE '08. New York, NY, USA: ACM.

Jonsson, S., Waern, A., Montola, M., & Stenros, J. (2007, June). Game mastering a pervasive larp. experiences from Momentum. In *Proceedings of the 4th international symposium on pervasive gaming applications* (pp. 31–39). Salzburg, Austria: PerGames.

Kasapakis, V., Gavalas, D., & Bubaris, N. (2013). Pervasive games research: a design aspects-based state of the art report. In *Proceedings of the 17th panhellenic conference on informatics* (pp. 152–157). New York, NY, USA: ACM.

Koleva, B., Taylor, I., Benford, S., Fraser, M., Greenhalgh, C., Schnädelbach, H., ... Adams, M. (2001). Orchestrating a mixed reality performance. In *Proceedings of the SIGCHI conference on human factors in computing systems* (pp. 38–45). New York, NY, USA: ACM.

Larsson, M. (2006, October). *Deliverable D9.8C: game design document – "geoquiz".*

Lim, M., Nijdam, N., & Magnenat-Thalmann, N. (2008, September). A general collaborative platform for mobile multi-user applications. In *Emerging technologies and factory automation, 2008. ETFA 2008. IEEE international conference on* (pp. 1346–1353). Hamburg, Germany: IEEE.

Magerkurth, C., Memisoglu, M., Engelke, T., & Streitz, N. (2004). Towards the next generation of tabletop gaming experiences. In *Proceedings of graphics interface 2004* (pp. 73–80). GI'04. Waterloo, Ontario, Canada: Canadian Human-Computer Communications Society.

Montola, M. (2012, September). *On the edge of the magic circle: understanding pervasive games and role-playing.* (Doctoral dissertation, School of Information Sciences).

Montola, M., Stenros, J., & Waern, A. (2009). *Pervasive games. theory and design. experiences on the boundary between life and play.* Burlington, MA, USA: Morgan Kaufmann Publishers.

Nieuwdorp, E. (2005). The pervasive interface: tracing the magic circle. In *Proceedings of digra 2005 conference: changing views – worlds in play.* Vancouver, Canada: DiGRA.

Nieuwdorp, E. (2007, April). The pervasive discourse: an analysis. *Computers in Entertainment (CIE), 5.*

Nokia. (2009, April). *Multi-user publishing environment (MUPE).* Retrieved from http://www.mupe.net

Oppermann, L. (2009, April). *Facilitating the development of location-based experiences.* (Doctoral dissertation, The University of Nottingham).

Paelke, V., Oppermann, L., & Reimann, C. (2008). Mobile location-based gaming. In *Map-based mobile services- design, interaction and usability* (Chap. 15, pp. 310–334). Springer Berlin Heidelberg.

Papakonstantinou, S., & Brujic-Okretic, V. (2009). Prototyping a context-aware framework for pervasive entertainment applications. In *Games and virtual worlds for serious applications, 2009. VS-GAMES'09. conference in* (pp. 84–91). Coventry, UK: IEEE.

Peitz, J., Saarenpää, H., & Björk, S. (2007). Insectopia: exploring pervasive games through technology already pervasively available. In *Proceedings of the international conference on advances in computer entertainment technology* (pp. 107–114). ACE '07. New York, NY, USA: ACM.

Rashid, O., Mullins, I., Coulton, P., & Edwards, R. (2006). Extending cyberspace: location based games using cellular phones. *Computers in Entertainment (CIE), 4* (1), 4.

Rogers, Y., Price, S., Harris, E., Phelps, T., Underwood, M., Wilde, D., ... Michaelides, D. T. (2002, February). *Learning through digitally-augmented physical experiences: reflections on the ambient wood project.*

Sanneblad, J., & Holmquist, L. E. (2003). Opentrek: a platform for developing interactive networked games on mobile devices. In *Human-computer interaction with mobile devices and services* (pp. 224–240). Udine, Italy: Springer Berlin Heidelberg.

Sanneblad, J., & Holmquist, L. E. (2004). "why is everyone inside me?!" using shared displays in mobile computer games. In *Entertainment computing – ICEC 2004* (pp. 487–498). Eindhoven, The Netherlands: Springer Berlin Heidelberg.

Schilit, B., Adams, N., & Want, R. (1994). Context-aware computing applications. In *Mobile computing systems and applications, 1994. WMCSA 1994. first workshop on* (pp. 85–90). Santa Cruz, California, USA: IEEE.

See, B. L. (2001, October). *Elvin interface for LambdaMOO*. (Master's thesis, University of Queensland).

Söderlund, T. (2009). Digital cityscapes. (Chap. Proximity Gaming: New Forms of Wireless Networking Gaming, pp. 217–250). USA: Peter Lang.

Ståhl, O., Drozd, A., Greenhalgh, C., & Koivisto, A. (2006, August). *Deliverable D6.7: second phase release of the IPerG platforms*.

Ståhl, O., Ohlenburg, J., Greenhalgh, C., & Nenonen, V. (2007, August). *Deliverable D6.8: final release of the IPerG platforms*.

Stenros, J., Montola, M., Waern, A., & Jonsson, S. (2007, May). *Deliverable D11.8 appendix c: momentum evaluation report*.

Suomela, R., Räsänen, E., Koivisto, A., & Mattila, J. (2004). Open-source game development with the multi-user publishing environment (MUPE) application platform. In *Entertainment computing – ICEC 2004* (pp. 308–320). Eindhoven, The Netherlands: Springer Berlin Heidelberg.

Thomas, B., Close, B., Donoghue, J., Squires, J., De Bondi, P., Morris, M., & Piekarski, W. (2000). Arquake: an outdoor/indoor augmented reality first person application. In *Wearable computers, the fourth international symposium on* (pp. 139–146). Atlanta, GA, USA: IEEE.

Thompson, M. K., Weal, M. J., Michaelides, D. T., Cruickshank, D. G., & Roure, D. C. D. (2003). *MUD slinging: virtual orchestration of physical interactions*. ECSTRIAM03-007.

Trinta, F., Ferraz, C., & Ramalho, G. (2006). Middleware services for pervasive multiplatform networked games. In *Proceedings of 5th ACM SIGCOMM workshop on network and system support for games* (p. 39). New York, NY, USA: ACM.

Waern, A., Bichard, J. P., Boss, E., & Åkesson, K.-P. (2008, February). *Deliverable D14.3: game design description, integrated game description*.

Waern, A., Lindt, I., Wetzel, R., & Åkesson, K.-P. (2008, April). *Deliverable D14.5: final version of boxes and the internally produced game*.

Yahyavi, A., & Kemme, B. (2013). Peer-to-peer architectures for massively multiplayer online games: a survey. *ACM Computing Surveys (CSUR), 46* (1), 9.

Chapter 3
Case Study: Virtual World Engine Staging a Pervasive Game

3.1 Choosing a Candidate Engine to Repurpose

Different types of game engines have been mentioned in Sect. 1.2 and a feature set to support pervasive games has been distilled and verified in Chap. 2. Because the feature set requires support for a virtual game world with world persistence, and a shared data space with data persistence, a virtual world engine is chosen as primary candidate for, being an engine in the same product line as a would-be pervasive game engine. As proof-of-concept, a specific virtual world engine implementation is extended to support the entire feature set and used to implement the pervasive game, called Codename: Heroes (CN:H). In this chapter, an explanatory case study (Johannesson & Perjons, 2014) is presented validating the chosen architecture and giving needed first-hand experience with the resulting architecture. Whereas features from the survey inform the architecture, the implementation of CN:H serves to highlight those features of particular importance and identify any open issues. Before dividing into technical details, the design aspects of CN:H are provided first.

3.2 Codename: Heroes

Codename: Heroes was to be developed in-house and due to limited resources needed the benefits of rapid development. From the outset, CN:H was specified to be a 'long term pervasive game', spanning months or years. The game world was said to overlap both the physical and virtual i.e., satisfying the sub-domain criteria. CN:H was designed to make explicit use of game mastering, both in day-to-day operation and specially designed weekend events. The game client, depicted in Fig. 3.1, was designed to be a prop 'in the mythos' (Jonsson & Waern, 2008) of the game. The

© The Author(s) 2015   41
K.J.L. Nevelsteen, *A Survey of Characteristic Engine Features*
for Technology-Sustained Pervasive Games, SpringerBriefs in Computer Science,
DOI 10.1007/978-3-319-17632-1_3

Fig. 3.1   Two screenshots of the game client, designed in the mythos of the game; the large circular area is designed to communicate the player's 'mana' level

game client was developed to the point of fully functional prototype. Further details on CN:H, from a cultural perspective, can be found in the works by Back and Waern (2013, 2014).

3.3   The Architecture

The specific virtual world engine implementation chosen, and centerpiece of the CN:H architecture (see Fig. 3.2), is the LambdaMOO (MOO) engine, by Pavel Curtis (MOO, 2012); a descendent in the family of MUD[1] architectures (collectively denoted as MU*/MOO), which can be traced back to the original virtual world implementation of 1978, called MUD1 (Bartle, 2003). The MOO engine stands as centralized server to all heterogenous devices. Only one game server was utilized, but with the idea that the centralized server could be expanded to multiple servers later. The centralized server is directly connected to non-volatile storage; for MOO this storage is a flat file, but a relational database is a common alternative approach.

---

[1]It is possible to trace the relation of MUD to pervasive games back to at least 2001. According to Nieuwdorp (2007), the first time the word 'pervasive' was used in conjunction with 'gaming' was by Falk (2001), where MUD was considered "a virtual counterpart to LARP". It is through the shared trait of world persistence that pervasive games have been said to be a direct descendant of MUD (de Souza e Silva & Sutko, 2009a).

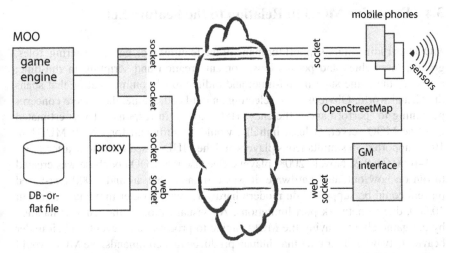

Fig. 3.2 CN:H software architecture: game engine connected to a database or flat file; networking of game engine with proxy and mobile phones through the Internet; mobile phones have sensors sensing the physical world; proxy connected via Web Sockets to the GM interface via the Internet; and, GM interface connected via the Internet to OpenStreetMap

To connect to the MOO server, clients can communicate via either the Telnet or MCP protocols (see Sect. 3.4.3 below). The game client was a fully functional Java-based mobile phone application, running on an Android-OS enabled smartphone, which is programmed to speak directly to the MOO engine. The mobile application opens a socket to and through the Internet to connect to the listening socket of the MOO server. Synchronization of local data with the server and possible disconnects are responsibilities of game client. Through sensors on the mobile phone (e.g., GPS, camera and accelerometer) the game client could interact with the physical world (e.g., the crowd-sourced artifacts, see Sect. 3.4.1 below).

An additional client to the game engine that was created, is the browser-based game mastering tool, for a GM to monitor player movement and activity. The GM tool is an OpenStreetMap WebMap implemented using HTML5 and Javascript, accessible via any web enabled computer or smartphone. The GM tool was a prototype precursor to the game master interface work by Guerrero Corbi (2014). To allow the web-based GM tool to connect to MOO, a small proxy server was created, which offered WebSocket (Fette & Melnikov, 2011) connectivity to the GM tool and simultaneously connected to MOO via Telnet and MCP (see Sect. 3.4.3 below). Essentially the proxy was an easy way to translate between HTML and MCP protocols.

## 3.4	Pervasive MOO in Relation to the Feature Set

MOO has rudimentary support for many of the features e.g., game mastering; roles, groups, hierarchies and permissions; content creation and scripting in run-time; access to the game state in run-time; and bidirectional communication that spans the virtual world. Obviously, by selecting an outdated engine, there were concerns pertaining to 'performance efficiency' (ISO, 2011). In response, it was estimated that one MOO server, at least initially, would be sufficient for CN:H; MUD1 in 1978 supported 36 simultaneous players and the MUD-based Gemstone after 1987, 650–1000 (Hall & Novak, 2008) players. Because the MOO codebase was created to run on now outdated hardware, it was estimated that around 3,000 text-based players could be supported on modern hardware, with a outer maximum of about 20,000, due to network port limitations. All visualization in the game is handled by the game client, leaving the MOO engine to process game events, albeit under heavier network load; rather than human produced text commands, the MOO would process game client events with sensor data.

### 3.4.1	Virtual Game World with World Persistence

MOO maintains a spatiotemporal world instance that retains player data seemingly indefinitely. CN:H has three different types of game elements that exist virtually in the MOO instance. First, crowd-sourcing was used to generate artifacts i.e., players built their own physical game elements, using virtual 'blueprints', which were assigned a unique identifier, in the form of an optically readable code (QR-code). These QR-codes could be read by the game client, to link the physical game object to its virtual counterpart (see Fig. 3.3). In this way, the game world overlapped with both the virtual and physical. Second, the players themselves, were also assigned a virtual game object that is linked to their game client, giving them presence in the virtual world. And third, a primary mechanic in CN:H was for players, or teams of players, to carry virtual messages towards specific goals. Messages were virtual game objects, without a physical counterpart, that were either virtually contained in an artifact or carried by players virtually. Both virtual messages and artifacts had an 'implied location' (Rashid, Mullins, Coulton, & Edwards, 2006) i.e., the location of a message or artifact had a location relative to, the player carrying or container holding, the artifact.

During the months or years that CN:H was planned to run, the game world would need to be ubiquitously available to the player, supporting temporal expansion. At any time of the day, a player would be able to turn on the game client and access the virtual game world i.e., the client could access the game server ubiquitously, requiring game engine reliability. MOO is proven to be reliable (i.e., mature, available, fault tolerant and recoverable (ISO, 2011)), through a long standing heritage of open-source community maintenance (Bartle, 2003).

Fig. 3.3 Player scanning a physical object via its QR-code, to access its virtual counterpart

3.4.2 Shared Data Space(s) with Data Persistence

To provide a shared data space, the architecture for CN:H was initially conceived as client software running on a smartphone connecting to one or more centralized servers. MOO provides a shared data space for CN:H, and coordinates network communication from different clients to it. MOO periodically persists the world's data space, which resides in memory, to non-volatile storage, reloading the world in the event of system failure. Some issues with MOO are that: Holding all world data in memory simultaneously and periodically persisting it to a flat file is an outdated practice. Clients are responsible for their own data persistence. In the event of client failure, it is the client's responsibility to synchronize game state with the game engine. Another disadvantage of MOO is its inability to scale over more than one server, but considering the limited number of players initially, this was not considered an immediate problem. The MOO architecture could be expanded later e.g., the MUD-based engine running EverQuest was extended to handle 400,000 players distributed across at least 40 servers (Bartle, 2003).

3.4.3 Heterogeneous Devices and Systems

The game client and the GM tool were both created to provide ubiquity of access to the virtual game world while participants were on the move. Heterogeneity between the game client and the GM tool was extensive, differing in hardware type, operating system, programming languages and network protocols. In itself, MOO does not support heterogeneous devices. Originally MOO was designed to be accessed simultaneously by many players, each through a networked computer running a Virtual Terminal program and the Telnet protocol (Postel & Reynolds, 1983). As MUD clients became more diverse and elaborate, an extension to Telnet, called MUD Client Protocol (MCP) (MOO, 2012), was devised to support more elaborate and differing game clients.

MCP makes use of a concept called 'out-of-band data' (MOO, 2012) which seemingly splits the network communication channel in two, by escaping control messages[2] between client and server, allowing for asynchronous remote procedure calls on a channel hidden from the player. To effectively communicate via MCP, client and server must first negotiate a common interface beforehand. A disadvantage of the outdated MCP extension, is that although the engine can support many custom interfaces, all are linked to a single player login object, with MOO asserting the player is logged-in from only one device i.e., no support for crossmedia. This turned out to be a problem for game masters who wanted to access the GM tool, but were still also logged in via Virtual Terminal to access the game state. To work around this issue, a ghost player was created to handle a second incoming connection from a game master.

In CN:H, MCP formed part of the device abstraction layer to support the game client and GM tool. MCP proved sufficient for the game client, because the client could be programmatically controlled not to drop connections during times of uncertain connectivity. For the GM tool, however, because the HTML5 protocol is commonly connectionless, the proxy running alongside MOO provided a constant connection to the MOO. Via the proxy, MOO could access service-oriented architectures or provide its own services. In this sense, the proxy is part of the device abstraction layer, translating web protocols into MCP calls. To populate the WebMap on the GM tool, geographical data from OpenStreetMap is accessed as a web service and location data is accessed as MCP calls routed via WebSockets. The same communication technique was being considered to add social networking to CN:H, in the next iteration of development.

Although flexible, MCP does not fully resolve interoperability issues between heterogeneous devices and services e.g., one protocol has been agreed upon in advance, connectionless transmission is not supported and the need for stateless

---

[2]Escaping (or control signaling) is prefixing a message with a special marker so that it can be identified and handled differently i.e., as a control message.

transactions is not questioned. In this case, the implementation of CN:H raised awareness to assumptions that were made during the design phase, highlighting how critical the problem of interoperability is.

It is difficult to say with which service-oriented systems a pervasive game engine should be combined. It could be argued that all pervasive games make use of geographical data and therefore would benefit from being combined with a GIS or map data from OpenStreetMap. Context information is needed, so a constant connection with a wireless sensor network could also be argued for. Because of the prevalence of the Internet, it can also be argued that a game engine needs to be combined with a web server by default as well. In any case, the ability for a game engine to interface with other systems is important.

3.4.4 Context-Awareness

To obtain a degree of context-awareness in CN:H, each participant carried a smartphone running a copy of the game client. The game client could access the smartphone sensor and actuator hardware (e.g., 3G, GPS, Bluetooth, accelerometers, vibration motor), and communicate with the game engine via mobile networking, using asynchronous remote procedure calls. Note that 3G and Bluetooth are also sensors, because they can be used for position triangulation (de Souza e Silva & Sutko, 2009b) and proximity detection, respectively. Additionally, because the client maintained a nearly constant connection with the game server, when the player was online, player presence and activity could be detected, with inactive players being marked as 'idle'. Usage of context-awareness in CN:H was rather limited, using only position tracking and proximity. To allow for GPS-based positioning the MOO engine needed to be modified to support a different spatial model (Nevelsteen, 2014). The original MOO virtual world consists of a number of 'room' nodes with a directed graph between them. In CN:H, GPS position coordinates were added to relevant game objects, rather than use the room-based nodes. Player GPS coordinates were updated through position localization and the implied location of other objects equated to the player's position, whenever a player interacted with an object. Each GPS snapshot links a virtual game object to a particular location (Nevelsteen, 2014). Although the engine supported it, the design of CN:H explicitly avoided the need for detecting a player in a bounded area. Additional context information in CN:H, was the geographical data surrounding active players, provided for by the GM tool by OpenStreetMap. Other potential sources of context information, not used in CN:H, were GIS data, social media, or any information on the Internet e.g., see (Suomela, Räsänen, Koivisto, & Mattila, 2004).

Due to the mobile nature of the game, uncertainty had to be dealt with, both in position localization and degradation of mobile networking. The Telnet protocol (Postel & Reynolds, 1983) used by MOO was an advantage in the mobile setting, because as long as the connection was not explicitly closed, long periods of inactivity did not negate the connection.

3.4.5 Roles, Groups, Hierarchies, Permissions

MOO already supported roles for participants, including the ability to sort them into groups and hierarchies; a group being a 'collection object' holding other objects and each new hierarchy being a branch on the main MOO game object hierarchy. MOO provides three different participant roles by default: `player`, `programmer` and the all powerful `wizard` role. Groups were used to allow collections of players to venture through quests collectively i.e., a collection object, holding the group of players, could be tied to different quest stages and different timestamps (Nevelsteen, 2014). Hierarchies were used for classification e.g., determining the required permission level needed in order to interact with the various game objects. Each game object has associated owner and permission flags, to control if and how other roles are able to interact with the object e.g., the combination of roles and permissions were used to limit access to MCP functionality. Roles and permissions determined what actions game participants could take, including actions taken through GM tools. Aside from object properties, MOO allows one or more run-time scripts to be attached to each game object, each with their own associated owner and permissions, allowing for almost any additional functionality to be added to a game object. The all powerful `wizard` role ignores permission flags, granting wizards the ability to make any modification to the system, even those leading to catastrophic events in MOO. The three basic MOO roles, plus the additionally created role of `game_master`, were used in CN:H. Although not ideal, the permission system was sufficient. Implementing additional permission flags would have required invasive modification to the engine.

The game design included plans to outsource some GM responsibilities to advanced players (called 'Sages'), effectively crowd-sourcing the human resources needed to stage the game. But, due to time constraints, the feature was not implemented. Creating the role of `sage` would have meant deriving the role from the `game_master` role and reducing it's permissions.

3.4.6 Current and Historical Game State

The minimal world configuration (called a 'core' (MOO, 2012)) that can be loaded into the MOO data space, does not require any player information; each game object, including the player object, is assigned and identified by an auto-incremented number during creation. The core that was expanded on in CN:H is called JHCore (MOO, 2012) and requires, as player information, a name and password. Additional player information specific to CN:H was added to the player game object e.g., bluetooth identifier, email address, 'mana', 'available rituals' and 'available blueprints'.

Each game object (including it's identifier, permissions, parent object, properties and associated scripts) is encoded in a text format in the MOO data space. The data space is stored in memory and directly accessible to those with permission, via the command line interface of a Virtual Terminal. Thus, a wizard can access the entire world state in the data space and optionally export it to storage i.e., all game data could be logged. Logging provided a historical view of game state e.g., turning GPS coordinates into GPS trails. Unfortunately, support for advanced logging, such as streaming data, was lacking in MOO. After each staging of CN:H, a post-game analysis was performed, including questionnaires and log analysis. Results of the analysis was for research purposes and to incrementally improve the game design.

MOO supports a system for documenting that was sufficient for CN:H, but with the drawback that, it did not support any data types other than text e.g., binary data such as images or sound. Documentation detailing how to use questing was created in the documentation system, but since the stagings of CN:H were with a relatively small number of participants, the documentation system was not used to pass information between game masters.

3.4.7 Game Master Intervention

Because providing game mastering requires a large amount of resources (Thompson, Weal, Michaelides, Cruickshank, & Roure, 2003; Flintham et al., 2003), most virtual worlds are designed to run fully automatic, with only a minority of worlds being semi-automatic or fully game mastered role-playing worlds (Bartle, 2003). Therefore the MOO architecture features only rudimentary game mastering tools e.g., to aid players who have technical issues or social conflicts within the world.

CN:H was designed to run semi-automatic; mostly automatic during day-to-day operation, but with certain events being flagged for game master intervention, and the possibility for fully game mastered role-playing events during weekends. For a game master to be able to effectively intervene in a running stream of events, a mechanism needed to be in place to: stop an event and all progression dependent on that event; signal a game master that a decision was needed; and resume progression according to the GM's decision or according to a default value, after a timeout. In CN:H, progress in the game was represented as progression through stages of a quest. MOO room nodes were used to represent quest stages and the graph between them represented all possible progressions through the quest. To implement GM intervention, an 'intervention bit' was added to each room game object i.e., each quest stage. If the bit was set, a script associated with the quest stage would execute, checking conditions to see whether a game master needed to be notified. The GM intervention bit was implemented and tested as proof-of-concept, but was never tested during play.

No specialized game master interface was considered at design time. A GM interface could be either implemented directly in MOO (with access to the entire game state e.g., including any roles or permissions), or MOO could provide a selection of the game state through web services for a third party GM interface, using the proxy described previously. Initially MOO's text-based command interface was used for all game mastering and MOO allows direct alteration of the entire game state in run-time. Advanced CN:H specific GM commands were created in MOO's run-time scripting language e.g., performing a series of basic commands or translating event data into a consumable form. After the initial play testing, the versatility of MCP was fully understood and the minimalistic GM tool (the OpenStreetMap WebMap) was implemented for the role of `game_master`, as a visualization of virtual objects and their GPS locations. After the second staging of CN:H, a Master's Degree project was carried out to "develop a generic architecture for interfaces of game-masters of pervasive games that allows adaptability" (Guerrero Corbi, 2014).

3.4.8   Reconfiguration, Authoring and Scripting in Run-Time

The MOO virtual world engine is designed to run continuously, so the phases of pre- and in-game are one and the same; any functionality available pre-game was available in-game also. By tying the game mechanics to game object locations, rather than specific physical locations, CN:H strived to obtain location adaptability. In run-time, but still pre-game quests could be created or altered to suit a specific staging. Once in-game, modifications could be made, but care had to be taken not to disrupt the game in progress i.e., special weekend events could still be created leaving the day-to-day mechanics undisturbed.

A major reason to choose the MOO implementation was specifically because it fulfilled the requirement of run-time content creation and scripting, described by Bartle (2003) as highly dynamic. The run-time scripting language in MOO is called MUD Object-Oriented; the 'fully expressive' scripting language, created by Stephen White in 1990, was created enabling users to create beyond what was originally imagined by the original MOO developers (Bartle, 2003). Content authoring in run-time, was used in CN:H, to allow for content to be crowd-sourced e.g., players were allowed to create personal artifacts that could be imported into the game. One caveat encountered was that, content creation that requires change in the physical world, without an actuator to bring about that change, is impossible. This became apparent at the design time of CN:H e.g., how can CN:H create virtual game objects with a physical counterpart, with potentially massive amounts of players spread all over the world? A solution is to "hack into reality" (Jonsson & Waern, 2008); tie existing phenomena from the physical world into the game world. Crowd-sourced player artifacts were coupled to a virtual object via generated and printed QR-codes. 3D scanning of physical objects was considered, but QR-codes were chosen because they were simpler to implement. A similar caveat applies to run-time content creation in combination with heterogeneous devices. Although, the game engine supports run-time content creation, game clients wanting to make use of new content, have to support dynamic content also. MCP solved inconsistencies between client and server when dealing with an all text-based content. But, if content has dependencies that can only be resolved at compile time (e.g. thick clients), new run-time content on the client side is limited to what the existing framework supports (Bell, 2007). An option is to use HTML or other markup language, but it is not a complete solution since not since all types of content can be represented. This again highlights an interoperability problem.

CN:H was implemented entirely using scripting language, without the need to recompile the engine code. The scripting language supports autonomous agents and was used to create the NPC called `void_walker`. Because scripting is done in run-time, so is debugging. This made the entire virtual world a continuous simulation where the WOz technique could be used to simulate game play prior to staging. All game elements in the physical world had a virtual counterpart that could be manipulated to simulate player interaction.

3.4.9 Bidirectional Diegetic and Non-diegetic Communication

Unless players deliberately choose another medium (e.g., to limit communication disclosure (Bergström, 2011)), all communication in MOO is intended to stay within the virtual world. The chat communication channel is bi-directional and can be used for both diegetic and non-diegetic purposes. MOO features a mail system for de-layed communication and a news channel for uni-directional communication to the players in the virtual world. Since players in CN:H are playing in the physical world and not continually behind a stationary computer screen, communication mediums in MOO were not sufficient. The graphical user interface, sensors and actuators on the game client/smartphone, provided for partial diegetic communication (e.g., through blinking lights, accelerometer readings or haptic vibration feedback), but the main uni-directional diegetic channel was achieved by extending the MOO mail system into the game client. Although MOO supports a bi-directional chat system, the game client did not provide access to it. Using the client as an non-diegetic bi-directional communication channel was decided against, as not to break the mythos of the game i.e., the presence of a non-diegetic channel would most likely reduce the fiction surrounding the game client. Due to limited development resources, no alternative was created for non-diegetic communication, and so this defaulted to email and phone conversations i.e., soft events that could not be picked up by the engine.

3.5   Discussion

To summarize, MOO and its extensions (including MCP) supported the feature set from the survey, with most of the work revolving around engineering interoperability. All changes implementing CN:H, including interoperability via MCP, were scriptable in the run-time scripting language; no engine code was modified i.e., indicating that the engine was an appropriate choice. It was, however, felt that more commonly used scripted functionality (e.g., those routines responsible for geodesic distances and triangulation) should be moved to the engine, providing easier access to common functionality and better performance, by being implemented in a compile time language.

As of this writing, Codename: Heroes has been publicly successfully staged twice in the area of Stockholm, Sweden, with no issues from the game architecture. CN:H as proof-of-concept seems to indicate that a virtual world engine, supporting the resulting feature set, could be successfully repurposed to stage a pervasive game. In no way is MOO an ideal engine, given the problems, caveats and disadvantages outlined in each of the feature sections above, but the case study seems to underline that MOO is at least in the same product line as a would-be pervasive game engine.

References

Back, J., & Waern, A. (2013). "we are two strong women" – designing empowerment in a pervasive game. In *DiGRA 2013 - defragging game studies*. Atlanta, GA, USA: DiGRA.

Back, J., & Waern, A. (2014). Codename Heroes–designing for experience in public places in a long term pervasive game. In *Proceedings of the 9th international conference on the foundations of digital games*. Ft. Lauderdale, FL, USA: Foundations of Digital Games.

Bartle, R. (2003). *Designing virtual worlds*. Indianapolis, Indiana, USA: New Riders Publishing.

Bell, M. (2007). *Guidelines and infrastructure for the design and implementation of highly adaptive, context-aware, mobile, peer-to-peer systems*. (Doctoral dissertation, University of Glasgow, Faculty of Information and Mathematical Sciences, Department of Computing Science).

Bergström, K. (2011). Framing storytelling with games. In *Interactive storytelling* (pp. 170–181). Lecture Notes in Computer Science. Vancouver, Canada: Springer Berlin Heidelberg.

de Souza e Silva, A., & Sutko, D. M. (2009a). Digital cityscapes. (Chap. Merging Digital and Urban Playspaces: An introduction to the Field, pp. 1–20). USA: Peter Lang.

de Souza e Silva, A., & Sutko, D. M. (Eds.). (2009b). *Digital cityscapes*. USA: Peter Lang.

Falk, J. (2001). MUD nexus: the world as game board for computer games. In *CHI2001, workshop on distributed and disappearing user interfaces in ubiquitous computing*.

Fette, I., & Melnikov, A. (2011, December). *IETF tools: the websocket protocol: RFC6455*. Retrieved from http://tools.ietf.org/html/rfc6455

Flintham, M., Benford, S., Anastasi, R., Hemmings, T., Crabtree, A., Greenhalgh, C., ... Row-Farr, J. (2003, April). Where on-line meets on the streets: experiences with mobile mixed reality games. In *Proceedings of the SIGCHI conference on human factors in computing systems* (pp. 569–576). CHI '03. New York, NY, USA: ACM.

Guerrero Corbi, V. (2014, July). *Development of a web based interface for game-masters of pervasive games*. (Master's thesis, Universitat Politècnica de Catalunya).

Hall, R., & Novak, J. (2008, April). *Game development essentials: online game development.* Clifton Park, NY, USA: Delmar Cengage Learning.

ISO. (2011). *ISO/IEC 25010:2011 systems and software engineering – systems and software quality requirements and evaluation (SQuaRE) – system and software quality models.*

Johannesson, P., & Perjons, E. (2014). *An introduction to design science.* Springer International Publishing Switzerland.

Jonsson, S., & Waern, A. (2008). Art of game-mastering pervasive games, the. In *Proceedings of the 2008 international conference on advances in computer entertainment technology* (pp. 224–231). ACE '08. New York, NY, USA: ACM.

MOO. (2012). *LambdaMOO (official site).* Retrieved from http://www.moo.mud.org

Nevelsteen, K. J. L. (2014, September). Applying GIS concepts to a pervasive game: spatiotemporal modeling and analysis using the Triad representational framework. *International Journal of Computer Science Issues, 11* (5).

Nieuwdorp, E. (2007, April). The pervasive discourse: an analysis. *Computers in Entertainment (CIE), 5.*

Postel, J., & Reynolds, J. (1983, May). *IETF tools: telnet: RFC854.* Retrieved from http://tools.ietf.org/html/rfc854

Rashid, O., Mullins, I., Coulton, P., & Edwards, R. (2006). Extending cyberspace: location based games using cellular phones. *Computers in Entertainment (CIE), 4* (1), 4.

Suomela, R., Räsänen, E., Koivisto, A., & Mattila, J. (2004). Open-source game development with the multi-user publishing environment (MUPE) application platform. In *Entertainment computing – ICEC 2004* (pp. 308–320). Eindhoven, The Netherlands: Springer Berlin Heidelberg.

Thompson, M. K., Weal, M. J., Michaelides, D. T., Cruickshank, D. G., & Roure, D. C. D. (2003). *MUD slinging: virtual orchestration of physical interactions.* ECSTRIAM03-007.

Chapter 4
Possible Extensions

4.1 Challenges and Open Issues

The problems, caveats and disadvantages mentioned (Sect. 3.4) in the case study serve to highlight challenges and open issues for the creation of a would-be pervasive game engine. These challenges include: (1) using distributed and decentralized architectures; (2) extending ubiquitous computing; (3) interoperability; and, (4) creating game master interfaces and tools.

4.1.1 Distributed and Decentralized Architectures

Exemplified by Demeure, Gentes, Stuyck, Guyot-Mbodji, and Martin (2008) (see also Sect. 2.3.2), fully decentralized architectures exist, where the game state is not centrally controlled and only shared with other clients when opportune. A challenge exists pertaining to the extent that a decentralized architecture can be utilized for games. Issues arise as how to: maintain security, maintain a shared data space and prevent cheating (Yahyavi & Kemme, 2013); gather and persist data (e.g., for monitoring); or, build dynamic user interfaces (see Sect. 3.4.8). To deal with the scalability issue in Sect. 3.4.2, virtual world engines already exist that use a centralized distributed system of servers for load balancing (BigWorld, 2014), so utilizing such techniques for pervasive games seems evident.

Possibly the most direct extension of the work contained in this book, would be to implement the feature set from the survey in a modern virtual distributed world engine (e.g., Big World Technology (BigWorld, 2014)), and analyze its ability as a pervasive game engine. Another approach being to analyze architectures of large scale pervasive games, based on distributed computing e.g., Ingress (Niantic Labs, 2014).

© The Author(s) 2015   55
K.J.L. Nevelsteen, *A Survey of Characteristic Engine Features*
for Technology-Sustained Pervasive Games, SpringerBriefs in Computer Science,
DOI 10.1007/978-3-319-17632-1_4

4.1.2   Extending Ubiquitous Computing

Devices and systems have the potential to offer richer context information for context-awareness e.g., the incorporation of body metrics or social relations. Ubiquitous computing remains a challenge, with open issues: increased utilization of context-awareness; reduction of soft events (e.g., in communication, see Sect. 3.4.9); focusing on technology that can be effectively pushed into the background (e.g., for ubiquity of access and diegetic communication); and, obtaining ubiquitous persona and presence (Dionisio, Burns III, & Gilbert, 2013) (see Sect. 3.4.3). The latter recognizing that a player's identity is made up of the sum of their interactions with the game e.g., crossmedia through different devices or interfaces. The amount of uncertainty in ubiquitous computing has been reduced considerably; early writings on pervasive games include much on mobile networking issues, which are solved in mainstream technologies today, but some issues are still critical e.g., losing connectivity by switching between WLAN and mobile networks. A partial solution could be that of delay-tolerate network communication, used in FinN (Akribopoulos et al., 2009), to obtain an eventually consistent game state in their distributed system.

4.1.3   Interoperability

A device abstraction layer is suggested in this book, but without a concrete design. In 2004, Greenhalgh, Izadi, Mathrick, Humble, and Taylor (2004) set out to interconnect heterogeneous devices with the EQUIP/ECT technologies. Broll, Ohlenburg, Lindt, Herbst, and Braun (2006) state *interoperability* in pervasive games to be a 'well-known problem'. And, a number of years later, Branton, Carver, and Ullmer (2011) dedicate an entire publication to deal with the 'important challenge' of interoperability through standardization. Many innovations, such as new languages or middleware, are sited by Branton et al. (2011) as partial solutions, but 'compatibility' (ISO, 2011) between web services was noted as 'largely lacking'. Since some game engines and service-oriented architectures are already distributed systems, and they interact (see Sect. 3.4.3), then interoperability is an issue between heterogeneous distributed systems as well i.e., similar to multi-cloud network communication (Singhal et al., 2013). Interoperability remains a challenge with the amount of heterogeneous devices and systems increasing and becoming more diverse.

4.1.4   Game Master Interfaces and Tools

This book discusses the challenge of building a reusable pervasive game engine. It seems reasonable to infer that reusable game master interfaces and authoring tools should also exist (e.g., see Broll et al. 2006). Some game master tools have already been created (e.g., for mobile games (Paelke, Oppermann, & Reimann, 2008) and authoring tools for location-based games (Oppermann, 2009)), but a more general reusable approach remains a challenge (Guerrero Corbi, 2014; Benford, Giannachi, Koleva, & Rodden, 2009) (see Sect. 3.4.7). Open issues are: capturing soft events and entering them in the game state; reducing the potential overload of data into a human consumable format; creating interfaces and visualizations that are applicable to a wide variety of games; and generating interfaces and visualizations that cater to the activity of game mastering rather than just presenting information.

4.2 Conclusion

That a game engine can be repurposed, has already been shown by Lewis and Jacobson (2002). To identify if a game engine could be repurposed to stage pervasive games (that make use of virtual game elements), a component feature set, for such an engine, has been distilled in the survey of Chap. 2. The feature set has been verified against the definitions of pervasive games and related work in Sect. 2.5. A virtual world engine has been selected, as candidate in the same product line as a would-be pervasive game engine in Sect. 3.4. To validate the resulting feature set and the chosen game engine, the pervasive game Codename: Heroes was implemented as proof-of-concept. CN:H was extended to support all features of the set. Although CN:H is not the first to implement a pervasive game using a virtual world engine (e.g., Ambient Wood (Thompson, Weal, Michaelides, Cruickshank, & Roure, 2003)), the production of CN:H gave needed first-hand experience, highlighting features of particular importance and any open issues. CN:H was successfully implemented, reaping the benefits of using the selected architecture; development time was low, spanning just a few months, with a third of the development resources spent on the game client. Although not all pervasive games will utilize all the features described, the aim is for the engine to support a wide variety of pervasive games. An additional aim for the feature set, is that it can be used to expand large scale virtual world engines into large scale pervasive game engines.

References

Akribopoulos, O., Logaras, M., Vasilakis, N., Kokkinos, P., Mylonas, G., Chatzigiannakis, I., & Spirakis, P. (2009). Developing multiplayer pervasive games and networked interactive installations using ad hoc mobile sensor nets. In *Proceedings of the international conference on advances in computer enterntainment technology* (pp. 174–181). New York, NY, USA: ACM.

Benford, S., Giannachi, G., Koleva, B., & Rodden, T. (2009). From interaction to trajectories: designing coherent journeys through user experiences. In *Proceedings of the SIGCHI conference on human factors in computing systems* (pp. 709–718). New York, NY, USA: ACM.

BigWorld. (2014). *Bigworld technology overview*. Retrieved from http://bigworldtech.com

Branton, C., Carver, D., & Ullmer, B. (2011). Interoperability standards for pervasive games. In *Proceedings of the 1st international workshop on games and software engineering* (pp. 40–43). New York, NY, USA: ACM.

Broll, W., Ohlenburg, J., Lindt, I., Herbst, I., & Braun, A.-K. (2006, October). Meeting technology challenges of pervasive augmented reality games. In *Proceedings of 5th ACM SIGCOMM workshop on network and system support for games* (p. 28). Singapore: ACM.

Demeure, I., Gentes, A., Stuyck, J., Guyot-Mbodji, A., & Martin, L. (2008). Transhumance: a platform on a mobile ad hoc network challenging collaborative gaming. In *Collaborative technologies and systems, 2008. CTS 2008. international symposium on* (pp. 221–228). Irvine, CA, USA: IEEE.

Dionisio, J. D., Burns III, W. G., & Gilbert, R. (2013). 3D virtual worlds and the metaverse: current status and future possibilities. *ACM Computing Surveys, 45* (3), 34:1–34:38.

Greenhalgh, C., Izadi, S., Mathrick, J., Humble, J., & Taylor, I. (2004, September). ECT: a toolkit to support rapid construction of ubicomp environments. In *Proceedings of workshop on system support for ubiquitous computing*. UbiSys. Nottingham, UK: Springer Verlag.

Guerrero Corbi, V. (2014, July). *Development of a web based interface for game-masters of pervasive games*. (Master's thesis, Universitat Politècnica de Catalunya).

ISO. (2011). *ISO/IEC 25010:2011 systems and software engineering – systems and software quality requirements and evaluation (SQuaRE) – system and software quality models*.

Lewis, M., & Jacobson, J. (2002, January). Game engines in scientific research. *Communications of the ACM, 45* (1), 27–31.

Niantic Labs. (2014). *Ingress*. Retrieved from https://www.ingress.com/

Oppermann, L. (2009, April). *Facilitating the development of location-based experiences*. (Doctoral dissertation, The University of Nottingham).

Paelke, V., Oppermann, L., & Reimann, C. (2008). Mobile location-based gaming. In *Map-based mobile services- design, interaction and usability* (Chap. 15, pp. 310–334). Springer Berlin Heidelberg.

Singhal, M., Chandrasekhar, S., Ge, T., Sandhu, R., Krishnan, R., Ahn, G.-J., & Bertino, E. (2013). Collaboration in multicloud computing environments: framework and security issues. *Computer, 46* (2), 76–84. doi:10.1109/MC.2013.46

Thompson, M. K., Weal, M. J., Michaelides, D. T., Cruickshank, D. G., & Roure, D. C. D. (2003). *MUD slinging: virtual orchestration of physical interactions*. ECSTRIAM03-007.

Yahyavi, A., & Kemme, B. (2013). Peer-to-peer architectures for massively multiplayer online games: a survey. *ACM Computing Surveys (CSUR), 46* (1), 9.

Appendix A
Surveyed Games and Technologies

A.1 Surveyed Pervasive Games

Bliin, *LOCUNET*, *CatchBob!*, *CityExplorer*, *CitySneak*, *Pac-Manhattan*, *MathX*, *Mystery Trip*, *Frequency 1550* (de Souza e Silva & Sutko, 2009); *Mogi* (de Souza e Silva & Sutko, 2009; Oppermann, 2009; Paelke, Oppermann, & Reimann, 2008); *Killer, The Beast, Shelby Logan's Run* (Montola, Stenros, & Waern, 2009), *Mystery on Fifth Avenue, Vem Gråter, The Amazing Race* (Montola et al., 2009); *Botfighters* (Montola et al., 2009; Oppermann, 2009); *REXplorer* (Montola et al., 2009; Oppermann, 2009; Ballagas, Kuntze, & Walz, 2008); *Geocaching, DefCon 10 WarDriving Contest, Noderunner* (Oppermann, 2009); *Love City* (Oppermann, 2009; Greenhalgh et al., 2007); *Riot! 1831* (Oppermann, 2009; Paelke et al., 2008); *Gunsliners, Swordfish, Forgotten Valley, Human Pacman* (Paelke et al., 2008); *NetAttack, TimeWarp* (Broll, Ohlenburg, Lindt, Herbst, & Braun, 2006); *URAY, CYSMN* (Sect. 2.2.1.1) (Flintham et al., 2003; Steve Benford et al., 2004; Steven Benford et al., 2006; Capra et al., 2005); *Ambient Wood* (Sect. 2.2.1.2) (de Souza e Silva & Sutko, 2009); *Treasure* (a.k.a. *Bill*) (Capra et al., 2005; Chalmers et al., 2005); *Feeding Yoshi* (Bell, Chalmers, et al., 2006) (Sect. 2.2.1); *Castles* (EQUATOR, 2010); *Day of the Figurines* (Broll et al., 2006; Flintham, Giannachi, Benford, & Adams, 2007); *Epidemic Menace* (Oppermann, 2009; Montola et al., 2009; Paelke et al., 2008; Broll et al., 2006); *Hitchers* (Oppermann, 2009; Capra et al., 2005; Drozd, Benford, Tandavanitj, Wright, & Chamberlain, 2006); *Prosopopeia Bardo 1 "Där vi föll"* (Jonsson, Montola, Waern, & Ericsson, 2006; Montola et al., 2009; IPerG, 2008); *Insectopia* (Peitz, Saarenpää, & Björk, 2007; Oppermann, 2009; Montola et al., 2009); *Geoquiz* (Larsson, 2006; IPerG, 2008); *Prosopopeia Bardo 2 "Momentum"* (Oppermann, 2009; Montola et al., 2009; Ståhl, Ohlenburg, Greenhalgh, & Nenonen, 2007; Waern, Lindt, Wetzel, & Åkesson, 2008; Hansson, Åkesson, & Wallberg, 2007; Jonsson, Waern, Montola, & Stenros, 2007); *Mythical: The Mobile Awakening (Mythical Mobile)* (Sect. 2.2.2.1); *Interference*

© The Author(s) 2015
K.J.L. Nevelsteen, *A Survey of Characteristic Engine Features*
for Technology-Sustained Pervasive Games, SpringerBriefs in Computer Science,
DOI 10.1007/978-3-319-17632-1

(Sect. 2.2.2.2); *Rider Spoke* (Oppermann, 2009); *The Node Game* (IPerG, 2008); *Backseat Playgrounds* (Bichard, Brunnberg, Combetto, Gustafsson, & Juhlin, 2006); *WeQuest* (Macvean et al., 2011); *Gopher Game* (Casey, Kirman, & Rowland, 2007); *Team Exploration* (Demeure, Gentes, Stuyck, Guyot-Mbodji, & Martin, 2008; Gentes, Guyot-Mbodji, & Demeure, 2010); *FreshUP* (Zender, Metzler, & Lucke, 2013; Kohlmann, Zender, & Lucke, 2012); *moBIO* (Segatto, Herzer, Mazzotti, Bittencourt, & Barbosa, 2008); *Supafly* (Jegers & Wiberg, 2006); *PAC-LAN* (Coulton, Bamford, Cheverst, & Rashid, 2008; Rashid, Mullins, Coulton, & Edwards, 2006); *False Prophets* (Mandryk & Maranan, 2002); *Tidy City* (Wetzel, Blum, & Oppermann, 2012); *Traveur* (Waern, Balan, & Nevelsteen, 2012); *AR-Quake* (Sect. 2.2.3) (Broll et al., 2006); and *Pac-Man Must Die!* (Sect. 2.2.4).

A.2 Surveyed Technologies

Mercury Platform (Oppermann, 2009); *Domino* (Bell, Hall, Chalmers, Gray, & Brown, 2006); *ECT* (Sect. 2.2.1.1); *Mixed Reality Toolkit (MRT)* (Freeman, 2004; EQUATOR, 2010); *Auld Linky* (MacColl et al., 2002); *EQUIP* (Sect. 2.2.1.1) (Greenhalgh et al., 2007; MacColl et al., 2002); *Elvin* (Sect. 2.2.1.2); *MUPE, WAF* (Sect. 2.2.2.1); *Morgan, PIMP, PART, Game Creator* (Sect. 2.2.2.2); *Log Analysis Tool* (Ståhl et al., 2007); *Mogile* (IPerG, 2008); *DotF Authoring Tool* (IPerG, 2008; Broll et al., 2006; Flintham et al., 2007); *Pooling Tool* (IPerG, 2008); *Transhumance* (Demeure et al., 2008; Paroux, Martin, Nowalczyk, & Demeure, 2007); *Pegasus* (Magerkurth, Engelke, & Grollman, 2006); *Mote* (Mottola, Murphy, & Picco, 2006); *Muddleware* (Wagner & Schmalstieg, 2007); *Middleware* (Ferreira, Orvalho, & Boavida, 2007); *Frap* (Tutzschke & Zukunft, 2009); *Player Space Director* (Hwang, Lee, Park, & Song, 2012); *Pervasive Multiplatform Multiplayer Game (PM2G)* (Trinta, Ferraz, & Ramalho, 2006); *STARS* (Sect. 2.2.6); *Fun in Numbers (FinN)* (Sect. 2.2.7); and *MARGE* (Chua, Goh, Lee, & Tan, 2010; Gu & Duh, 2011).

References

Ballagas, R., Kuntze, A., & Walz, S. P. (2008). Gaming tourism: lessons from evaluating rexplorer, a pervasive game for tourists. In *Pervasive computing* (pp. 244–261). Springer.

Bell, M., Chalmers, M., Barkhuus, L., Hall, M., Sherwood, S., Tennent, P., ... Hampshire, A. (2006). Interweaving mobile games with everyday life. In *Proceedings of the sigchi conference on human factors in computing systems* (pp. 417–426). CHI '06. Montréal, Québec, Canada: ACM. doi:10.1145/1124772.1124835

Bell, M., Hall, M., Chalmers, M., Gray, P., & Brown, B. (2006, May). Domino: exploring mobile collaborative software adaptation. In *Pervasive computing* (Vol. 3968, pp. 153–168). Lecture Notes in Computer Science. Dublin, Ireland: Springer Berlin Heidelberg.

Benford, S., Seager, W., Flintham, M., Anastasi, R., Rowland, D., Humble, J., ... Sutton, J. (2004). The error of our ways: the experience of self- reported position in a location-based game. In *Ubiquitous computing* (pp. 70–87). UbiComp 2004. Nottingham, UK: Springer Berlin Heidelberg.

Benford, S., Crabtree, A., Flintham, M., Drozd, A., Anastasi, R., Paxton, M., ... Row-Farr, J. (2006, March). Can You See Me Now? *ACM Transactions on Computer-Human Interaction (TOCHI), 13* (1), 100–133.

Bichard, J., Brunnberg, L., Combetto, M., Gustafsson, A., & Juhlin, O. (2006, September). Backseat playgrounds: pervasive storytelling in vast location based games. In *Entertainment computing – ICEC 2006* (pp. 117–122). Springer.

Broll, W., Ohlenburg, J., Lindt, I., Herbst, I., & Braun, A.-K. (2006, October). Meeting technology challenges of pervasive augmented reality games. In *Proceedings of 5th ACM SIGCOMM workshop on network and system support for games* (p. 28). Singapore: ACM.

Capra, M., Radenkovic, M., Benford, S., Oppermann, L., Drozd, A., & Flintham, M. (2005). The multimedia challenges raised by pervasive games. In *Proceedings of the 13th annual ACM international conference on multimedia* (pp. 89–95). ACM.

Casey, S., Kirman, B., & Rowland, D. (2007). The gopher game: a social, mobile, locative game with user generated content and peer review. In *Proceedings of the international conference on advances in computer entertainment technology* (pp. 9–16). ACM.

Chalmers, M., Bell, M., Brown, B., Hall, M., Sherwood, S., & Tennent, P. (2005, June). Gaming on the edge: using seams in ubicomp games. In *International conference on advances in computer entertainment technology* (pp. 306–309). New York, NY, USA: ACM.

Chua, A. Y., Goh, D. H., Lee, C.-S., & Tan, K.-T. (2010). Mobile alternate reality gaming engine: a usability evaluation. In *2010 seventh international conference on information technology* (pp. 540–545). Information Technology: New Generations (ITNG). IEEE.

Coulton, P., Bamford, W., Cheverst, K., & Rashid, O. (2008). 3D space-time visualization of player behaviour in pervasive location-based games. *International Journal of Computer Games Technology, 2*.

de Souza e Silva, A., & Sutko, D. M. (Eds.). (2009). *Digital cityscapes*. USA: Peter Lang.

Demeure, I., Gentes, A., Stuyck, J., Guyot-Mbodji, A., & Martin, L. (2008). Transhumance: a platform on a mobile ad hoc network challenging collaborative gaming. In *Collaborative technologies and systems, 2008. CTS 2008. international symposium on* (pp. 221–228). Irvine, CA, USA: IEEE.

Drozd, A., Benford, S., Tandavanitj, N., Wright, M., & Chamberlain, A. (2006). Hitchers: designing for cellular positioning. In *Ubicomp 2006: ubiquitous computing* (pp. 279–296). Springer.

EQUATOR. (2010, September). *EQUATOR Interdisciplinary Research Collaboration (IRC)*. Retrieved from http://web.archive.org/web/20100914131736/http://www.equator.ac.uk

Ferreira, P., Orvalho, J., & Boavida, F. (2007). A middleware architecture for mobile and pervasive large-scale augmented reality games. In *Communication networks and services research, 2007. CNSR'07. fifth annual conference on* (pp. 203–212). IEEE.

Flintham, M., Anastasi, R., Benford, S., Drozd, A., Mathrick, J., Rowland, D., ... Sutton, J. (2003, November). Uncle roy all around you: mixing games and theatre on the city streets. In *Level up conference proceedings*. University of Utrecht: DiGRA.

Flintham, M., Giannachi, G., Benford, S., & Adams, M. (2007, June). Day of the figurines: a slow narrative-driven game for mobile phones using text messaging. In *4th international symposium on pervasive gaming applications (PerGames)* (pp. 167–175). ICVS'07. Salzburg, Austria: Springer-Verlag.

Freeman, R. (2004, September). *Mixed reality toolkit, MSc VIVE final year project report*.

Gentes, A., Guyot-Mbodji, A., & Demeure, I. (2010). Gaming on the move: urban experience as a new paradigm for mobile pervasive game design. *Multimedia systems, 16* (1), 43–55.

Greenhalgh, C., Benford, S., Drozd, A., Flintham, M., Hampshire, A., Oppermann, L., ... von Tycowicz, C. (2007). Concepts and technologies for pervasive games, a reader for pervasive gaming research vol. 1. (Chap. EQUIP2: A Platform for Mobile Phone-based Game Development, Vol. 1, pp. 147–172). Shaker Verlag GmbH.

Gu, J., & Duh, H. B. (2011). Mobile augmented reality game engine. In *Handbook of augmented reality* (pp. 99–122). Springer.

Hansson, P., Åkesson, K.-P., & Wallberg, A. (2007, February). *Deliverable D11.9: second generation core platform.*

Hwang, I., Lee, Y., Park, T., & Song, J. (2012). Toward a mobile platform for pervasive games. In *Proceedings of the first ACM international workshop on mobile gaming* (pp. 19–24). ACM.

IPerG. (2008). *IPerG (integrated project on pervasive gaming) consortium.* Retrieved from http://iperg.sics.se

Jegers, K., & Wiberg, M. (2006). Pervasive gaming in the everyday world. *Pervasive Computing, IEEE, 5* (1), 78–85.

Jonsson, S., Montola, M., Waern, A., & Ericsson, M. (2006). Prosopopeia: experiences from a pervasive larp. In *Proceedings of the 2006 ACM SIGCHI international conference on advances in computer entertainment technology* (p. 23). ACE'06. New York, NY, USA: ACM.

Jonsson, S., Waern, A., Montola, M., & Stenros, J. (2007, June). Game mastering a pervasive larp. experiences from Momentum. In *Proceedings of the 4th international symposium on pervasive gaming applications* (pp. 31–39). Salzburg, Austria: PerGames.

Kohlmann, W., Zender, R., & Lucke, U. (2012). FreshUP—implementation and evaluation of a pervasive game for freshmen. In *Pervasive computing and communications workshops (PERCOM workshops), 2012 IEEE international conference on* (pp. 691–696). IEEE.

Larsson, M. (2006, October). *Deliverable D9.8C: game design document – "geoquiz".*

MacColl, I., Brown, B., Benford, S., Chalmers, M., Conroy, R., Dalton, N., ... Weal, M. (2002). Shared visiting in equator city. In *Proceedings of the 4th international conference on collaborative virtual environments* (pp. 88–94). New York, NY, USA: ACM.

Macvean, A., Hajarnis, S., Headrick, B., Ferguson, A., Barve, C., Karnik, D., & Riedl, M. O. (2011). WeQuest: scalable alternate reality games through end-user content authoring. In *Proceedings of the 8th international conference on advances in computer entertainment technology* (p. 22). ACM.

Magerkurth, C., Engelke, T., & Grollman, D. (2006). A component based architecture for distributed, pervasive gaming applications. In *Proceedings of the 2006 ACM SIGCHI international conference on advances in computer entertainment technology* (p. 15). ACM.

Mandryk, R. L., & Maranan, D. S. (2002). False prophets: exploring hybrid board/video games. In *CHI'02 extended abstracts on human factors in computing systems* (pp. 640–641). ACM.

Montola, M., Stenros, J., & Waern, A. (2009). *Pervasive games. theory and design. experiences on the boundary between life and play.* Burlington, MA, USA: Morgan Kaufmann Publishers.

Mottola, L., Murphy, A. L., & Picco, G. P. (2006, October). Pervasive games in a mote-enabled virtual world using tuple space middleware. In *Proceedings of 5th ACM SIGCOMM workshop on network and system support for games.* Netgames. ACM.

Oppermann, L. (2009, April). *Facilitating the development of location-based experiences.* (Doctoral dissertation, The University of Nottingham).

Paelke, V., Oppermann, L., & Reimann, C. (2008). Mobile location-based gaming. In *Map-based mobile services- design, interaction and usability* (Chap. 15, pp. 310–334). Springer Berlin Heidelberg.

Paroux, G., Martin, L., Nowalczyk, J., & Demeure, I. (2007). Transhumance: a power sensitive middleware for data sharing on mobile ad hoc networks. In *7th international workshop on applications and services in wireless networks (aswn), santander, spain.*

Peitz, J., Saarenpää, H., & Björk, S. (2007). Insectopia: exploring pervasive games through technology already pervasively available. In *Proceedings of the international conference on advances in computer entertainment technology* (pp. 107–114). ACE '07. New York, NY, USA: ACM.

Rashid, O., Mullins, I., Coulton, P., & Edwards, R. (2006). Extending cyberspace: location based games using cellular phones. *Computers in Entertainment (CIE), 4* (1), 4.

Segatto, W., Herzer, E., Mazzotti, C. L., Bittencourt, J. R., & Barbosa, J. (2008). Mobio threat: a mobile game based on the integration of wireless technologies. *Computers in Entertainment (CIE), 6* (3), 39.

Ståhl, O., Ohlenburg, J., Greenhalgh, C., & Nenonen, V. (2007, August). *Deliverable D6.8: final release of the IPerG platforms.*

Trinta, F., Ferraz, C., & Ramalho, G. (2006). Middleware services for pervasive multiplatform networked games. In *Proceedings of 5th ACM SIGCOMM workshop on network and system support for games* (p. 39). New York, NY, USA: ACM.

Tutzschke, J.-P., & Zukunft, O. (2009). Frap: a framework for pervasive games. In *Proceedings of the 1st ACM SIGCHI symposium on engineering interactive computing systems* (pp. 133–142). ACM.

Waern, A., Balan, E., & Nevelsteen, K. J. L. (2012). Athletes and street acrobats: designing for play as a community value in parkour. In *Proceedings of the 2012 ACM annual conference on human factors in computing systems* (pp. 869–878). CHI '12. Austin, Texas, USA: ACM. doi:10.1145/2207676.2208528

Waern, A., Lindt, I., Wetzel, R., & Åkesson, K.-P. (2008, April). *Deliverable D14.5: final version of boxes and the internally produced game.*

Wagner, D., & Schmalstieg, D. (2007). Muddleware for prototyping mixed reality multiuser games. In *Virtual reality conference, 2007. VR'07. IEEE* (pp. 235–238). IEEE.

Wetzel, R., Blum, L., & Oppermann, L. (2012). Tidy city: a location-based game supported by in-situ and web-based authoring tools to enable user-created content. In *Proceedings of the international conference on the foundations of digital games* (pp. 238–241). ACM.

Zender, R., Metzler, R., & Lucke, U. (2013). FreshUP—a pervasive educational game for freshmen. *Pervasive and Mobile Computing.*

Index

© The Author(s) 2015
K.J.L. Nevelsteen, *A Survey of Characteristic Engine Features*
for Technology-Sustained Pervasive Games, SpringerBriefs in Computer Science,
DOI 10.1007/978-3-319-17632-1

Printed in the United States
By Bookmasters